Intelligence Convergence

Designing Governance for the AI–IoT Ecosystem

By

Amir Jahangir

Amir Jahangir

Amir Jahangir is an influential author and public intellectual whose writings focus on the intersection of technology, policy, and governance. With a career spanning over two decades in strategic communications and public policy design, he has authored numerous thought-provoking articles and reports published by the World Economic Forum, Hilal Magazine, LinkedIn, and Narratives Magazine, among others.

Amir's most recent contribution as a chapter author in the book Mapping Governance Innovations: Perspectives from South Asia (Routledge, 2024) highlights his pioneering work in aligning Artificial Intelligence (AI) and Media and Information Literacy (MIL) with governance frameworks in Pakistan. His chapter examines how anticipatory governance models can address complex socio-technological challenges through innovation-led reforms.

As a trained AI policy strategist from Harvard University and a design thinker from Stanford, Amir brings a unique blend of technical insight and governance acumen to his writing. His narratives explore how AI can enhance institutional efficiency, transparency, and resilience, particularly in developing economies.

Amir's written work reflects a forward-thinking approach grounded in practical experience. He is the Editor of the Governance Accountability Index, which serves as a vital tool for policymakers and researchers alike. His writing continues to shape discourse around emerging technologies and their impact on the future of public administration and citizen engagement.

Table of Contents

Foreword

In an age defined by exponential change, the convergence of Artificial Intelligence (AI) and the Internet of Things (IoT) signals not just a technological evolution, but a fundamental reconfiguration of governance, economy, and society. Intelligence Convergence: Navigating AI-IoT Integration in Policy Design is a timely and consequential work that offers a compelling blueprint for policymakers, institutional leaders, and global strategists seeking to navigate this new frontier.

Amir Jahangir—whose leadership in innovation, public policy, and systemic design thinking is recognized globally—has authored a book that is more than a theoretical exploration; it is a strategic response to one of the defining challenges of our time. His vision is grounded in lived experience, policy acumen, and an unwavering commitment to ensuring that technological advancement aligns with societal values.

The integration of AI and IoT is reshaping every layer of decision-making—from smart cities and autonomous logistics to predictive healthcare and digitally-augmented governance. As billions of devices come online and algorithms begin to make decisions previously reserved for humans, the role of policy must evolve from static regulation to dynamic stewardship.

Jahangir argues convincingly for the establishment of adaptive governance frameworks—regulatory architectures that are anticipatory, interoperable, and agile enough to respond to rapid innovation cycles. The book articulates the risks of regulatory lag and digital exclusion while providing practical pathways to ensure that policy frameworks remain inclusive, ethical, and future-fit.

What emerges is a call for a new class of leadership—leaders who possess:

- Multidisciplinary fluency: Understanding how emerging technologies interface with legal, social, economic, and ethical domains.
- Systemic foresight: The ability to anticipate long-term implications across interconnected systems
- Collaborative competence: Engaging citizens, industry, academia, and civil society in co-creating policy solutions
- Resilience thinking: Building governance structures capable of absorbing shocks and adapting to volatility
- Human-centered stewardship: Placing dignity, trust, and public interest at the heart of AI-IoT deployment.

This book also serves as a critical bridge between the global North and South, spotlighting the unique policy imperatives and opportunities for emerging economies. From Pakistan's digital transformation agenda to global debates on ethical AI, Intelligence Convergence presents a framework that is both locally relevant and globally scalable.

For international institutions, regulators, development agencies, and forward-looking governments, this book offers an actionable guide to shaping policy that not only keeps pace with innovation but ensures it delivers shared prosperity, security, and justice.

As we stand at the precipice of the intelligence era, our challenge is clear: to govern technologies that will increasingly govern us. Amir Jahangir has provided us with the intellectual tools, strategic frameworks, and moral compass to rise to this moment.

Dr. Gulfam Baghoor

Policy Strategist | Global Futurist | Advisor to Governments and Multilateral Institutions

April 2025

Making Connectivity as a Decision Making Tool

Making connectivity a decision-making tool involves leveraging the seamless integration of devices, data, and networks to enhance decision-making processes. In today's interconnected world, the fusion of AI and IoT enables real-time data collection and analysis from a multitude of sources, creating a comprehensive view of complex systems. This connectivity allows decision-makers to access relevant information instantaneously, enabling more informed, data-driven decisions. By utilizing the continuous flow of data from connected devices, organizations can anticipate trends, identify patterns, and respond proactively to emerging challenges. In essence, connectivity transforms decision-making from a reactive process into a proactive, informed strategy, enhancing efficiency, accuracy, and adaptability across various sectors.

Policymakers need to develop a robust policy design around the integration of AI and IoT to navigate the complexities and harness the full potential of this technological convergence. As AI enhances IoT systems with advanced data analytics, real-time decision-making, and predictive capabilities, the volume of data generated by interconnected devices is growing exponentially. This presents both opportunities and challenges. Without a well-defined policy framework, the risks related to data privacy, security, and ethical considerations could outweigh the benefits, leading to mistrust, misuse, and potential harm. A thoughtfully crafted policy can mitigate these risks by establishing clear guidelines on data management, ethical AI use, and system interoperability, ensuring that the technology serves the public good while fostering innovation.

Each stakeholder stands to benefit significantly from such a policy framework. For governments, a regulated environment will enhance national security by setting standards for data protection and cybersecurity, reducing vulnerabilities to attacks and breaches. It also provides a legal foundation to address issues of liability and accountability in the event of AI-IoT system failures. Industry players, on the other hand, can benefit from a level playing field where standardized protocols and regulations promote fair competition and innovation. With clear guidelines, businesses and research can operate with greater confidence, knowing that their investments in AI-IoT technologies are safeguarded by robust legal protections.

Consumers and civil society will also enjoy increased trust in AI-IoT systems, knowing that their data is protected and used ethically. Policies that emphasize transparency, consent, and fairness will empower individuals to make informed choices about how their data is used, thus enhancing user engagement and satisfaction. Furthermore, ethical guidelines embedded in the policy design can prevent biases and discrimination in AI decision-making, ensuring that these technologies contribute positively to societal welfare.

By developing a comprehensive policy design around AI-IoT integration, policymakers can create an ecosystem where stakeholders enjoy the liberty to operate and innovate while benefiting from the wealth of data generated by IoT devices. This balance between regulation and freedom is crucial for fostering an environment where technological advancements align with societal values, ultimately leading to a more efficient, secure, and equitable future.

Introduction

The rapid convergence of Artificial Intelligence (AI) and the Internet of Things (IoT) is reshaping the technological and societal landscape, creating a new paradigm where intelligent systems and connected devices collaborate to drive innovation across various sectors. Generating data from each action and reaction in the system. This convergence, often referred to as "Intelligence Convergence," is more than a mere technical advancement; it represents a fundamental shift in how data is collected, analyzed, and utilized to make decisions. As AI enhances IoT systems with capabilities like real-time data analysis, predictive analytics, and autonomous decision-making, these technologies are becoming increasingly integral to the infrastructure of modern society.

From healthcare and smart cities to manufacturing and transportation, the integration of AI and IoT is unlocking unprecedented opportunities for efficiency, automation, and innovation. However, alongside these opportunities come significant challenges that demand the attention of policymakers. The sheer volume of data generated by IoT devices, combined with the autonomous decision-making power of AI, raises complex issues related to data privacy, security, ethics, and governance. These challenges are not merely technical; they are deeply intertwined with societal values, requiring a nuanced and forward-thinking approach to policy design.

This book, **"Intelligence Convergence: Navigating AI-IoT Integration in Policy Design,"** seeks to explore the multifaceted implications of this technological convergence on public policy and regulatory frameworks. It aims to provide a comprehensive examination of the challenges and opportunities presented by AI-IoT integration and propose strategies for developing adaptive policy frameworks that align technological advancements with societal needs and public interests.

In the pages that follow, we will delve into the technological aspects of AI-IoT convergence, highlighting the sectors most impacted and presenting case studies that illustrate real-world applications. We will then shift our focus to the policy challenges that arise from this integration, addressing critical issues such as data privacy, ethical considerations, regulatory compliance, and the complexities of liability and accountability. The book will also explore strategies for policymakers to navigate these challenges effectively, emphasizing the importance of adaptive, collaborative, and ethical policy frameworks.

By the end of this book, readers will have a deeper understanding of the profound impact of AI-IoT convergence on policy design and the crucial role that policymakers play in ensuring that these technologies serve the greater good. The goal is to equip policymakers, researchers, and industry stakeholders with the knowledge and tools needed to navigate the intersection of AI and IoT in a way that fosters innovation while safeguarding societal values.

Overview of AI and IoT

Before we dive into the policy implications of AI-IoT convergence, it is helpful to provide a brief overview of these two technologies and how they are reshaping the world. Artificial intelligence (AI) refers to the ability of machines or software to perform tasks that normally require human intelligence, such as reasoning, learning, perception, decision making, and natural language processing. Internet of things (IoT) refers to the network of physical devices, sensors, and actuators that are embedded with computing capabilities and connected to the Internet, enabling them to collect, process, and exchange data. Both AI and IoT have experienced rapid growth and development in recent years, driven by advances in hardware, software, cloud computing, and communication technologies.

AI and IoT are complementary technologies that can enhance each other's capabilities and create new value propositions. On one hand, AI can augment IoT by providing intelligent analysis, prediction, and optimization of the data generated by IoT devices, as well as enabling natural and intuitive human-machine interactions. On the other hand, IoT can augment AI by providing rich and diverse data sources, real-time feedback, and distributed computing power for AI algorithms. The integration of AI and IoT can thus enable smarter, faster, and more efficient solutions for a wide range of domains, such as smart cities, smart homes, smart health, smart agriculture, smart manufacturing, smart mobility, and smart energy. The convergence of AI and IoT can also enable new forms of human-machine collaboration, such as digital assistants, social robots, and augmented or virtual reality.

According to a report by McKinsey, the potential economic impact of AI-IoT convergence could reach $11.1 trillion per year by 2025, accounting for about 11% of global GDP (The Ineternet of Things: Mapping the Value Beyond the Hype 2015, McKinsey Global Institute).[1] However, this technological convergence also poses significant challenges and risks for public policy and governance, as it raises complex and interrelated issues such as data privacy, security, ethics, accountability, liability, regulation, and social inclusion. These issues require careful and coordinated policy responses that balance the interests and values of multiple stakeholders, such as governments, businesses, civil society, and consumers. Moreover, these policy responses need to be adaptive and flexible, as AI-IoT technologies are constantly evolving and creating new opportunities and threats. In the next section, we will examine some of the key sectors that are most impacted by AI-IoT convergence and present case studies that illustrate how these technologies are transforming various aspects of our lives.

Definition and basic concepts of AI and IoT

AI and IoT are two interrelated and rapidly evolving fields of technology that have the potential to transform various sectors and domains of human activity. In this section, we will provide some basic definitions and concepts of these technologies, as well as explain how they can complement and enhance each other.

AI is a broad term that encompasses multiple subfields and applications, such as machine learning, computer vision, natural language processing, speech recognition, robotics, and artificial neural networks. According to the European Commission, AI can be defined as "systems that display intelligent behavior by analyzing their

---

1   The Ineternet of Things: Mapping the Value Beyond the Hype 2015, McKinsey Global Institute: https://www.mckinsey.com/~/media/McKinsey/Industries/Technology%20Media%20and%20Telecommunications/High%20Tech/Our%20Insights/The%20Internet%20of%20Things%20The%20value%20of%20digitizing%20the%20physical

environment and taking actions – with some degree of autonomy – to achieve specific goals." (Artificial Intelligence for Europe, 2018). AI systems can perform tasks that normally require human intelligence, such as recognizing patterns, understanding natural language, solving problems, making decisions, and learning from data and experience. AI systems can also interact with humans and other machines in natural and intuitive ways, such as through voice, gestures, or emotions. AI systems can be classified into different types based on their level of autonomy, complexity, and generality, such as narrow AI, general AI, and super AI.

IoT is a term that refers to the network of physical objects, devices, sensors, and actuators that are embedded with computing capabilities and connected to the Internet or other networks, enabling them to collect, process, and exchange data. According to the International Telecommunication Union, IoT can be defined as "a global infrastructure for the information society, enabling advanced services by interconnecting (physical and virtual) things based on existing and evolving interoperable information and communication technologies." (ITU-T Recommendation Y.2060, 2012).

IoT devices can range from simple sensors and actuators, such as temperature sensors, motion detectors, or smart locks, to complex systems, such as smart phones, smart watches, smart cars, or smart drones. IoT devices can communicate with each other and with other systems, such as cloud servers, edge devices, or gateways, using various protocols and standards, such as Wi-Fi, Bluetooth, Zigbee, or 5G. IoT devices can also be integrated with other technologies, such as blockchain, big data, or cloud computing, to enable secure, scalable, and efficient data management and analytics.

AI and IoT are complementary technologies that can enhance each other's capabilities and create new value propositions. On one hand, AI can augment IoT by providing intelligent analysis, prediction, and optimization of the data generated by IoT devices, as well as enabling natural and intuitive human-machine interactions. For example, AI can help IoT devices to filter, compress, and aggregate data, as well as to extract useful insights and patterns from large and complex data sets. AI can also help IoT devices to adapt to changing environments, learn from feedback, and optimize their performance and efficiency.

Moreover, AI can help IoT devices to interact with humans and other devices in natural and intuitive ways, such as through voice, gestures, or emotions. For example, AI can enable IoT devices to understand natural language, recognize faces and emotions, and generate natural responses and actions. On the other hand, IoT can augment AI by providing rich and diverse data sources, real-time feedback, and distributed computing power for AI algorithms. For example, IoT devices can collect and transmit data from various physical and environmental contexts, such as temperature, humidity, sound, light, or motion, which can provide valuable inputs and outputs for AI systems.

IoT devices can also provide real-time feedback and evaluation for AI systems, such as through sensors, cameras, or microphones, which can help AI systems to improve their accuracy and reliability. Moreover, IoT devices can provide distributed computing power and storage for AI systems, such as through edge computing, fog computing, or swarm intelligence, which can help AI systems to reduce latency, bandwidth, and energy consumption.

The convergence of AI and IoT can thus enable smarter, faster, and more efficient solutions for a wide range of domains, such as smart cities, smart homes, smart health, smart agriculture, smart manufacturing, smart mobility, and smart energy. The convergence of AI and IoT can also enable new forms of human-machine collaboration, such as digital assistants, social robots, and augmented or virtual reality. However, this technological convergence also poses significant challenges and risks for public policy and governance, as it raises complex and interrelated issues such as data privacy, security, ethics, accountability, liability, regulation, and social inclusion. These issues require careful and coordinated policy responses that balance the interests and values of multiple stakeholders, such as governments, businesses, civil society, and consumers. Moreover, these policy responses need to be adaptive and flexible, as AI-IoT technologies are constantly evolving and creating new opportunities and threats. In the next section, we will examine some of the key sectors that are most impacted by AI-IoT convergence and present case studies that illustrate how these technologies are transforming various aspects of our lives.

Historical Context and Evolution of AI and IoT Technologies

The journey of Artificial Intelligence (AI) and the Internet of Things (IoT) technologies began decades ago, rooted in visionary concepts and incremental advancements that have shaped their evolution into the transformative forces they are today. The origins of AI can be traced back to the mid-20th century when pioneers like Alan Turing and John McCarthy laid the foundational theories of machine learning and computational intelligence. Turing's concept of a "universal machine" in the 1930s, capable of performing any computation, and McCarthy's coining of the term "Artificial Intelligence" in 1956 marked the beginning of AI as a distinct field of study.

The evolution of AI witnessed several phases, including the initial optimism of the 1950s and 1960s, the challenges and setbacks during the AI winters of the 1970s and 1980s, and the resurgence of interest in the 1990s with the advent of more powerful computing resources and data availability. Today, AI has progressed from rule-based systems to more sophisticated machine learning models, including neural networks and deep learning, enabling machines to perform complex tasks like natural language processing, image recognition, and autonomous decision-making.

Parallel to AI, the concept of interconnected devices, now known as the Internet of Things (IoT), began to take shape in the late 20th century. The idea of embedding sensors and actuators into physical objects was first explored in the early 1980s with projects like the Carnegie Mellon University's Coke machine, which was connected to the internet to report on its inventory status. However, it wasn't until the late 1990s and early 2000s, with the proliferation of wireless communication technologies and the expansion of the internet, that IoT began to gain significant traction.

The convergence of AI and IoT represents a natural progression in the evolution of these technologies. IoT devices generate vast amounts of data, which, when combined with AI, can be harnessed to create intelligent systems capable of real-time analysis and autonomous operation. This integration has opened up new possibilities across various sectors, from smart homes and cities to industrial automation and healthcare, revolutionizing how we interact with technology and the world around us.

The historical development of AI and IoT reflects a continuous process of innovation and adaptation, driven by technological advancements and the growing demand for smarter, more connected systems. As we move forward, understanding the historical context of these technologies is crucial for appreciating their current capabilities and envisioning their future potential.

The Regional and Global Progress in AI and IoT

The progress of AI and IoT technologies varies across different regions of the world, influenced by factors such as government policies, investment levels, infrastructure, and the availability of talent. An overview shows the United States leads with Europe following the suit of progress in key regions:

1. North America

- **United States:** The U.S. is a global leader in AI and IoT development, driven by strong government support, significant private sector investment, and a robust tech ecosystem. Major tech companies like Google, Microsoft, and Amazon are at the forefront of AI research, while IoT applications are widespread across industries like healthcare, manufacturing, and transportation. Initiatives such as the National AI Initiative Act and Smart Cities programs highlight the country's commitment to advancing these technologies.

- **Canada:** Canada has emerged as a hub for AI research, particularly in areas like machine learning and natural language processing. The country's AI strategy, launched in 2017, has led to the establishment of several AI institutes and partnerships with the private sector. IoT adoption is also growing, particularly in smart cities and agriculture.

2. Europe

- **Western Europe:** Countries like Germany, France, and the UK are key players in the AI and IoT landscape. Germany's focus on Industry 4.0 has made it a leader in industrial IoT, while France and the UK are investing heavily in AI research and development. The European Union's AI Act and Digital Strategy aim to create a regulatory framework that balances innovation with ethical considerations.

- **Eastern Europe:** The region is catching up, with countries like Estonia and Poland making strides in AI and IoT adoption. Estonia, known for its digital government initiatives, is leveraging AI for public services, while Poland is focusing on smart manufacturing and IoT in logistics.

3. Asia-Pacific

- **China:** China is rapidly becoming a global powerhouse in AI and IoT, driven by significant government investment and an ambitious national AI strategy. The country is advancing in areas like facial recognition, autonomous vehicles, and smart cities. IoT is widely used in manufacturing, agriculture, and urban development, with cities like Shenzhen leading the way in smart infrastructure.

- **Japan:** Japan has a strong focus on robotics and AI, particularly in the context of an aging population. The government's Society 5.0 initiative aims to integrate AI and IoT into society to address challenges like healthcare and transportation. Japan is also a leader in IoT applications in manufacturing, known as the Industrial Internet of Things (IIoT).

- **India:** India is emerging as a significant player in AI and IoT, with a growing tech ecosystem and government initiatives like Digital India. AI is being applied in areas such as healthcare, agriculture, and financial services, while IoT adoption is increasing in smart cities and industrial sectors.

- **Pakistan:** In Pakistan, the adoption of AI and IoT technologies is gradually taking shape, with increasing recognition of their potential to drive economic growth and enhance public services. The government has launched initiatives like the National AI Policy and the Digital Pakistan Vision, which aim to create a robust ecosystem for technological innovation. In sectors such as agriculture, AI and IoT are being utilized to optimize water usage, improve crop yields, and enhance supply chain efficiency. Urban areas like Karachi, Lahore, and Islamabad are witnessing a rise in tech startups focusing on AI-driven solutions for healthcare, education, and financial services. However, the country faces challenges in scaling these technologies due to infrastructure limitations, gaps in technical expertise, and the need for a supportive regulatory environment. Addressing these challenges through targeted investments in education, infrastructure, and policy reform will be crucial for Pakistan to fully harness the benefits of AI and IoT, contributing to national development and global competitiveness.

4. Middle East

- **United Arab Emirates (UAE):** The UAE is leading AI and IoT innovation in the Middle East, with the launch of the world's first AI strategy and initiatives like Smart Dubai, which aims to make Dubai the happiest and smartest city in the world. IoT is being used extensively in sectors like energy, transportation, and urban planning.

- **Saudi Arabia:** Saudi Arabia's Vision 2030 plan includes significant investment in AI and IoT, particularly in the development of smart cities like NEOM. The country is focusing on using these technologies to diversify its economy and improve public services.

5. Africa

- **South Africa:** South Africa is leading the continent in AI and IoT adoption, with a focus on sectors like agriculture, mining, and healthcare. The government is working on developing a national AI strategy, and there are several AI and IoT startups emerging in the region.

- **Nigeria:** Nigeria is making progress in AI and IoT, particularly in fintech and agriculture. The country's growing tech ecosystem and a young, tech-savvy population are driving innovation, although challenges like infrastructure and regulatory frameworks remain.

6. Latin America

- **Brazil:** Brazil is the leading country in Latin America for AI and IoT, with a focus on smart cities, agriculture, and manufacturing. The Brazilian government is investing in AI research and developing a national IoT plan to boost innovation and economic growth.

- **Mexico:** Mexico is also making strides in AI and IoT, particularly in manufacturing and logistics. The government's focus on Industry 4.0 is driving the adoption of these technologies in the country's industrial sector.

7. Oceania

- **Australia:** Australia is advancing in AI and IoT, with a focus on sectors like agriculture, mining, and smart cities. The Australian government has launched an AI Ethics Framework and is investing in research and development to position the country as a leader in these technologies.

The progress of AI and IoT technologies is uneven across the world, with developed regions like North America, Western Europe, and East Asia leading the way, while emerging economies in Africa, Latin America, and Southeast Asia are gradually catching up. Each region's approach to AI and IoT reflects its unique challenges and opportunities, and global collaboration will be key to realizing the full potential of these technologies.

The Concept of Intelligence Convergence

The concept of intelligence convergence refers to the integration of different forms of intelligence, such as human, artificial, and collective intelligence, to achieve higher levels of performance and innovation. The idea is that by combining the strengths and compensating for the weaknesses of each type of intelligence, new possibilities and solutions can emerge that would not be possible with any single type alone.

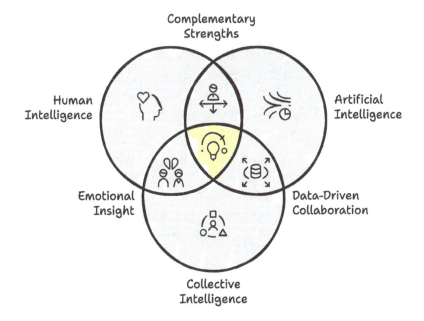

Synergy of Integrated Intelligence

Complementary Strengths

Human Intelligence

Artificial Intelligence

Emotional Insight

Data-Driven Collaboration

Collective Intelligence

The concept of intelligence convergence has historical roots in various fields and disciplines, such as cybernetics, artificial neural networks, human-computer interaction, collective intelligence, and cognitive science. Some of the early pioneers of this concept include Norbert Wiener, John von Neumann, Marvin Minsky, J.C.R. Licklider, Douglas Engelbart, and Howard Rheingold. They envisioned a future where humans and machines could cooperate and augment each other's capabilities through feedback loops, shared representations, and distributed cognition.

The concept also refers to the integration of Artificial Intelligence (AI) and the Internet of Things (IoT), resulting in the seamless interaction of smart devices, sensors, and AI algorithms. This convergence creates a network where data generated by IoT devices is processed, analyzed, and utilized by AI systems to enable intelligent decision-making, automation, and optimization across various sectors. The idea of intelligence convergence has been gaining traction as advancements in AI and IoT continue to reshape the technological landscape, offering new possibilities for innovation and efficiency.

To understand the concept of intelligence convergence, it is essential to trace the historical development of both AI and IoT technologies. AI, as a field of study, has its roots in the mid-20th century, with the pioneering work of computer scientists like Alan Turing and John McCarthy. Turing's development of the Turing Test in 1950 and McCarthy's coining of the term "artificial intelligence" in 1956 marked the beginning of a new era in computing. Early AI research focused on symbolic reasoning, problem-solving, and expert systems, which laid the foundation for more advanced machine learning techniques in later years.

Meanwhile, the concept of the Internet of Things can be traced back to the early 1980s when the idea of connecting physical objects to the internet was first proposed. The development of radio-frequency identification (RFID) technology in the 1990s further propelled the idea of interconnected devices, leading to the birth of the IoT. Kevin Ashton, a British technology pioneer, is credited with popularizing the term "Internet of Things" in 1999, envisioning a world where everyday objects could communicate and share data through a network.

As AI and IoT technologies evolved independently, their convergence became increasingly inevitable. The rise of big data, cloud computing, and advanced machine learning algorithms in the early 21st century provided the necessary infrastructure for AI and IoT to merge. The rapid proliferation of IoT devices, from smart home appliances to industrial sensors, generated vast amounts of data that required sophisticated analysis to derive meaningful insights. AI emerged as the key enabler for processing and analyzing this data, transforming raw information into actionable intelligence.

The convergence of AI and IoT gained momentum in the 2010s, as businesses and governments recognized the potential of combining these technologies to drive innovation and efficiency. Smart cities, autonomous vehicles, and industrial automation are just a few examples of how intelligence convergence has been applied in real-world scenarios. By integrating AI with IoT, these applications can leverage real-time data to make informed decisions, optimize processes, and enhance user experiences.

Theoretical Foundations of Intelligence Convergence

The theoretical foundations of intelligence convergence are rooted in the concepts of cyber-physical systems (CPS) and the Fourth Industrial Revolution (Industry 4.0). Cyber-physical systems refer to the integration of physical and digital components through a network, enabling real-time interaction and control. Industry 4.0, a term coined by the German government in 2011 and popularized by Professor Klaus Schwab, Founder and Executive Chairman of the World Economic Forum, is convinced that we are at the beginning of a revolution that is fundamentally changing the way we live, work, and relate to one another, which he explored in his new book, The Fourth Industrial Revolution. Which, represents the ongoing transformation of industries through the adoption of digital technologies, including AI, IoT, and automation (Schwab 2016)[2].

Intelligence convergence can be seen as an extension of these concepts, where AI serves as the cognitive layer that processes and interprets data generated by IoT devices. This cognitive layer allows for the automation of decision-making processes, the prediction of future trends, and the optimization of operations across various domains. The theoretical underpinnings of intelligence convergence emphasize the importance of data-driven intelligence, real-time responsiveness, and the seamless integration of digital and physical systems.

The convergence of AI and IoT has profound implications for various industries and sectors. In healthcare, for example, AI-driven IoT devices can monitor patients' vital signs in real-time, enabling early detection of potential health issues and personalized treatment plans. In

---

2   The Fourth Industrial Revolution, by Prof. Klaus Schwab 2016

manufacturing, intelligence convergence allows for predictive maintenance, where AI algorithms analyze data from IoT sensors to predict equipment failures and schedule timely repairs, minimizing downtime and reducing costs.

The implications of intelligence convergence extend beyond individual industries to broader societal and economic impacts. As AI and IoT become more integrated into everyday life, issues such as data privacy, security, and ethical considerations come to the forefront. Policymakers and regulators must navigate these challenges to ensure that the benefits of intelligence convergence are realized while minimizing potential risks.

The concept of intelligence convergence represents a significant milestone in the evolution of AI and IoT technologies. As these technologies continue to advance, their convergence will play a crucial role in shaping the future of industries, economies, and societies. The historical development of AI and IoT provides valuable insights into the trajectory of intelligence convergence, highlighting the importance of continued innovation, collaboration, and thoughtful policy design.

In recent years, intelligence convergence has gained renewed attention and relevance due to the rapid advances in AI and IoT technologies, as well as the emergence of new platforms and paradigms, such as cloud computing, big data, social media, and crowdsourcing. These developments have enabled new forms and scales of intelligence convergence, such as human-AI collaboration, swarm intelligence, augmented reality, and social machines. These phenomena pose both opportunities and challenges for society, as they reshape the roles and relationships between humans and machines, as well as among humans themselves.

Explanation of the Convergence Between AI and IoT.

The convergence between Artificial Intelligence (AI) and the Internet of Things (IoT) represents a transformative shift in how technology interacts with the world. At its core, this convergence involves the integration of AI's analytical and decision-making capabilities with the vast network of connected devices that constitute the IoT.

IoT refers to the network of physical objects—ranging from household appliances to industrial machines—that are embedded with sensors, software, and other technologies that enable them to connect and exchange data with other devices and systems over the internet. These devices generate enormous amounts of data in real-time, which can provide valuable insights if properly analyzed.

This is where AI comes into play. AI systems, particularly those utilizing machine learning, are designed to analyze complex datasets, recognize patterns, make predictions, and automate decisions. When AI is integrated with IoT, it can process the vast amounts of data generated by IoT devices, extract actionable insights, and even automate responses without human intervention.

For example, in a smart city, IoT sensors might monitor traffic flow, air quality, and energy usage in real-time. AI systems can analyze this data to optimize traffic light patterns, suggest alternative routes to reduce congestion, or adjust energy distribution to meet demand. Similarly, in a smart home, IoT devices like thermostats and security cameras can be managed by AI, learning user preferences over time to optimize comfort and security while reducing energy consumption.

This convergence creates a symbiotic relationship where IoT provides the data, and AI provides the intelligence to make sense of it. The result is a more responsive, efficient, and intelligent system capable of making real-time decisions that improve processes, enhance user experiences, and solve complex problems.

The convergence of AI and IoT also leads to the creation of intelligent ecosystems. These ecosystems can range from smart homes and cities to industrial automation and healthcare systems. The real-time data from IoT devices, combined with AI's ability to learn and adapt, can lead to the development of autonomous systems that can make decisions with minimal human intervention.

Importance of Convergence in the Modern Technological Landscape.

The convergence of AI and IoT holds paramount importance in the modern technological landscape, as it marks the evolution from isolated smart devices to interconnected, intelligent systems capable of transforming industries, economies, and daily life. This convergence addresses the growing need for efficiency, automation, and real-time decision-making in an increasingly complex world.

In industries such as manufacturing, this integration enables predictive maintenance, reducing downtime and enhancing productivity by allowing machines to anticipate and resolve issues before they escalate. In healthcare, AI and IoT together create advanced monitoring systems that provide continuous patient data, enabling more personalized and timely care interventions. Smart cities benefit from this convergence through optimized resource management—like energy distribution, traffic flow, and waste management—resulting in reduced operational costs and improved quality of life for residents.

Moreover, the convergence supports the development of innovative business models, such as servitization, where companies offer products as services based on real-time data and AI-driven insights. This shift not only enhances customer satisfaction but also creates new revenue streams and competitive advantages.

On a broader scale, the importance of AI and IoT convergence lies in its potential to address global challenges such as climate change, urbanization, and resource scarcity. By enabling smarter energy grids, efficient water management systems, and sustainable agricultural practices, this convergence can contribute significantly to achieving sustainability goals.

The migration from IPv4 to IPv6, along with the ongoing evolution of AI and IoT technologies, necessitates the development of a robust governance framework to ensure seamless communication between Internet Protocols and devices, both in close proximity and across vast distances. As the number of connected devices grows exponentially, the complexities of managing their interactions in various mediums and layers also increase. A governance framework is essential to standardize protocols, ensure interoperability, and manage the security and privacy of data exchanged between devices. This framework must address the diverse range of communication environments—whether they involve short-range connections within a smart home or long-range interactions across global networks.

For devices to communicate effectively, the governance framework should include rules and guidelines that cover all layers of communication, from the physical network layer to the application layer. This includes establishing standards for data formats, communication protocols, and security measures that can be universally applied. Additionally, the framework should incorporate mechanisms for real-time monitoring and management, allowing for the dynamic adjustment of policies and protocols as new technologies emerge and network conditions change.

Moreover, the governance framework needs to accommodate the various types of networks and mediums through which devices communicate, such as wired, wireless, and satellite networks. It should provide clear guidelines on how devices in different environments can interoperate, ensuring that they can exchange data efficiently and securely, regardless of their underlying infrastructure.

This governance framework must be adaptable to the global nature of IoT and AI systems, which often involve devices operating under different regulatory environments and standards. International cooperation and harmonization of standards will be crucial in facilitating the smooth interaction of devices across borders, ensuring that the benefits of AI-IoT convergence can be realized on a global scale. By establishing such a framework, policymakers can help create a more resilient and interoperable technological ecosystem, where devices can communicate seamlessly, enhancing the overall efficiency and effectiveness of AI-IoT systems.

Relevance to Policy Design

Incorporating the convergence of AI and IoT into policy design requires a shift from traditional infrastructure-centric or data-centric approaches to a more human-centered framework. As AI-IoT integration increasingly influences various aspects of daily life, policy must prioritize the needs, rights, and well-being of individuals and communities, ensuring that technological advancements serve people rather than merely optimizing resources or infrastructure.

A people-centric policy approach focuses on the ethical implications, social impacts, and equitable access to the benefits of AI and IoT technologies. For instance, while AI-driven IoT systems can enhance public services like healthcare, transportation, and urban management, policy must ensure that these technologies are deployed in ways that respect privacy, protect data security, and avoid reinforcing existing inequalities. By placing individuals at the core of policy design, policymakers can address concerns such as surveillance, algorithm bias, and accessibility, ensuring that the deployment of AI-IoT solutions benefits all segments of society.

Moreover, a people-centric policy framework encourages the development of adaptive, transparent, and accountable governance structures. It calls for multi-stakeholder engagement, where citizens, communities, and civil society organizations actively participate in shaping the policies that govern AI-IoT technologies. This approach fosters trust and social acceptance, which are critical for the successful adoption of new technologies.

By contrast, infrastructure-centric or data-centric policies risk prioritizing efficiency and optimization over human welfare, potentially leading to scenarios where technology outpaces society's ability to manage its ethical and social ramifications. For example, focusing solely on data maximization might overlook the privacy concerns of individuals whose data is being collected and processed. Similarly, an infrastructure-centric approach might prioritize the deployment of smart systems in urban areas, inadvertently widening the digital divide between urban and rural communities.

The Necessity of Policy Frameworks to Manage AI-IoT Integration.

The integration of AI and IoT, often referred to as Intelligence Convergence, presents unprecedented opportunities for innovation, efficiency, and improved quality of life. However, these advancements also come with complex challenges that require robust policy frameworks to manage effectively. As AI-IoT systems become more pervasive, their influence extends into critical sectors such as healthcare, transportation, energy, and urban management. The necessity for comprehensive policy frameworks to govern this integration is, therefore, paramount.

Firstly, the rapid pace of AI-IoT adoption outstrips the existing regulatory and legal structures in many parts of the world. Without updated policies, there is a risk of legal ambiguity, where the deployment of AI-IoT technologies could lead to unintended consequences, such as breaches in privacy, data security, and even civil liberties. For instance, AI-driven IoT devices that collect vast amounts of personal data require stringent regulations to prevent misuse and ensure that data protection standards are upheld. In this context, policy frameworks serve as the bedrock for setting clear guidelines on data ownership, privacy rights, and the ethical use of AI technologies.

Secondly, policy frameworks are essential to fostering innovation while ensuring public safety and trust. AI-IoT integration brings significant benefits, such as enhanced decision-making, predictive analytics, and automation of routine tasks. However, these benefits must be balanced with the need to mitigate risks such as cybersecurity threats, system failures, and ethical concerns. Policies that promote transparency, accountability, and inclusivity in AI-IoT deployment can help build public trust and ensure that these technologies are developed and used responsibly.

Moreover, a well-structured policy framework can provide a competitive advantage at the national level. Countries that proactively develop and implement policies for AI-IoT integration are better positioned to lead in the global digital economy. These frameworks can help standardize practices across industries, facilitate international cooperation, and attract investment in AI and IoT sectors. Additionally, policies that encourage research and development, as well as public-private partnerships, can drive innovation and ensure that AI-IoT technologies contribute to economic growth.

Lastly, policy frameworks are crucial for ensuring that the benefits of AI-IoT integration are equitably distributed across society. Without deliberate policy interventions, there is a risk that these technologies could exacerbate existing inequalities, leaving certain communities or regions behind. Policies that promote digital inclusion, such as providing access to technology and digital literacy programs, are essential to ensuring that all individuals and communities can participate in and benefit from AI-IoT advancements.

Technological Convergence of AI and IoT with the Role of IPv6, Blockchain, and Global Standardization

The technological convergence of Artificial Intelligence (AI) and the Internet of Things (IoT) represents a significant shift in how devices connect, communicate, and make decisions autonomously. This convergence brings together the data-gathering capabilities of IoT with the analytical and decision-making power of AI, enabling more intelligent and adaptive systems. At the core of this evolution is the transition from IPv4 to IPv6, a necessary advancement to accommodate the growing number of IoT devices and the data they generate.

IPv4 vs. IPv6 and the Future of Internet Protocols:

IPv4 (Internet Protocol version 4) has been the standard for internet communications since the early days of the internet. However, with only about 4.3 billion unique addresses available, IPv4 has reached its limit, which poses significant challenges in an era where billions of devices are connected to the internet. IPv6 (Internet Protocol version 6) was developed to address this limitation, offering an almost infinite number of unique IP addresses (approximately 3.4×10^{38} addresses). Besides providing more addresses, IPv6 also introduces improvements in routing and network autoconfiguration, making it more suitable for the modern internet and the expansive growth of IoT devices. The future beyond IPv6 is still speculative, but it might involve more sophisticated networking models, possibly integrating quantum networking principles or advanced, decentralized systems supported by blockchain technologies.

Role of IPv6 in AI-IoT Convergence:

The adoption of IPv6 is crucial for the continued expansion and efficiency of IoT networks. IPv6 not only supports a vast number of devices but also enhances security features, which are paramount in a world where IoT devices collect and transmit sensitive data. The additional address space in IPv6 allows for better device management and tracking, which is critical when AI algorithms require precise and secure data to function effectively. Moreover, IPv6 facilitates the deployment of AI-powered IoT systems in environments where IPv4 would struggle due to address exhaustion, such as in densely populated urban areas or industrial settings with extensive automation.

Global Standardization Challenges and Regional Differences:

The migration from IPv4 to IPv6 has not been uniform across the globe, with significant differences between regions. In the US and Europe, the transition has been gradual but consistent, driven by policy support and industry cooperation. However, China and similar countries have taken a more aggressive approach, aiming to lead in the adoption

of IPv6. China's rapid expansion of its internet infrastructure and IoT networks has necessitated a swift shift to IPv6, which aligns with its ambitions to dominate in AI and IoT technologies. This has also led to differences in how standards are developed and implemented. While the US and Europe typically follow a more consensus-driven approach to standardization, China has often pursued its own standards, which can sometimes create compatibility challenges globally. As AI and IoT systems increasingly require cross-border integration, these differences in standardization approaches could lead to technical and geopolitical complexities.

Blockchain and Emerging Technologies in Standardization:

Blockchain technology is increasingly seen as a potential solution to some of the challenges posed by the divergence in standards and the need for secure, decentralized systems. Blockchain can provide a decentralized framework for managing IoT devices, ensuring that data is securely exchanged and authenticated across different networks, regardless of the underlying standards. For example, blockchain can enable smart contracts that automatically enforce rules and agreements between devices from different manufacturers or operating in different jurisdictions, facilitating smoother interoperability. Additionally, other emerging technologies, such as edge computing and quantum cryptography, may also play roles in establishing new standards that are more flexible and resilient than current protocols.

In conclusion, the convergence of AI and IoT is driving significant advancements in how we interact with technology, with IPv6 playing a crucial role in supporting this growth. The transition from IPv4 to IPv6 is essential for accommodating the expanding IoT landscape and ensuring that AI systems can operate effectively. However, global differences in standardization approaches, particularly between China and Western countries, present challenges that need to be addressed through international cooperation and the adoption of new technologies like blockchain. As we move toward a future where billions of devices are interconnected and intelligent, the establishment of robust, flexible, and secure standards will be critical in realizing the full potential of AI-IoT convergence.

Global Standardization Challenges and Regional Differences:

The migration from IPv4 to IPv6 has not been uniform across the globe, with significant differences between regions. In the US and Europe, the transition has been gradual but consistent, driven by policy support and industry cooperation. However, China and similar countries have taken a more aggressive approach, aiming to lead in the adoption of IPv6. China's rapid expansion of its internet infrastructure and IoT networks has necessitated a swift shift to IPv6, which aligns with its ambitions to dominate in AI and IoT technologies.

This has also led to differences in how standards are developed and implemented. While the US and Europe typically follow a more consensus-driven approach to standardization, China has often pursued its own standards, which can sometimes create compatibility challenges globally. As AI and IoT systems increasingly require cross-border integration, these differences in standardization approaches could lead to technical and geopolitical complexities.

Blockchain and Emerging Technologies in Standardization:

Blockchain technology is increasingly seen as a potential solution to some of the challenges posed by the divergence in standards and the need for secure, decentralized systems. Blockchain can provide a decentralized framework for managing IoT devices, ensuring that data is securely exchanged and authenticated across different networks, regardless of the underlying standards. For example, blockchain can enable smart contracts that automatically enforce rules and agreements between devices from different manufacturers or operating in different jurisdictions, facilitating smoother interoperability. Additionally, other emerging technologies, such as edge computing and quantum cryptography, may also play roles in establishing new standards that are more flexible and resilient than current protocols.

The convergence of AI and IoT is driving significant advancements in how we interact with technology, with

IPv6 playing a crucial role in supporting this growth. The transition from IPv4 to IPv6 is essential for accommodating the expanding IoT landscape and ensuring that AI systems can operate effectively. However, global differences in standardization approaches, particularly between China and Western countries, present challenges that need to be addressed through international cooperation and the adoption of new technologies.

The migration from IPv4 to IPv6, along with the ongoing evolution of AI and IoT technologies, necessitates the development of a robust governance framework to ensure seamless communication between Ineternet Protocols (IPs) and devices, both in close proximity and across vast distances. As the number of connected devices grows exponentially, the complexities of managing their interactions in various mediums and layers also increase.

A governance framework is essential to standardize protocols, ensure interoperability, and manage the security and privacy of data exchanged between devices. This framework must address the diverse range of communication environments—whether they involve short-range connections within a smart home or long-range interactions across global networks.

For devices to communicate effectively, the governance framework should include rules and guidelines that cover all layers of communication, from the physical network layer to the application layer. This includes establishing standards for data formats, communication protocols, and security measures that can be universally applied. Additionally, the framework should incorporate mechanisms for real-time monitoring and management, allowing for the dynamic adjustment of policies and protocols as new technologies emerge and network conditions change.

Moreover, the governance framework needs to accommodate the various types of networks and mediums through which devices communicate, such as wired, wireless, satellite networks, and other possible future modes of communications. It should provide clear guidelines on how devices in different environments can interoperate, ensuring that they can exchange data efficiently and securely, regardless of their underlying infrastructure.

The governance framework must be adaptable to the global nature of IoT and AI systems, which often involve devices operating under different regulatory environments and standards. International cooperation and harmonization of standards will be crucial in facilitating the smooth interaction of devices across borders, ensuring that the benefits of AI-IoT convergence can be realized on a global scale. By establishing such a framework, policymakers can help create a more resilient and interoperable technological ecosystem, where devices can communicate seamlessly, enhancing the overall efficiency and effectiveness of AI-IoT systems.

The Inevitability of Policy Frameworks to Manage AI-IoT Integration.

To effectively manage the integration of AI and IoT, robust policy frameworks are essential. These frameworks are needed to guide the development and deployment of AI-IoT systems, ensuring they operate in a manner that is safe, secure, and beneficial to society. As AI and IoT technologies continue to converge, they present new challenges related to both personal and data privacy, security, ethical use, and the equitable distribution of technological benefits. A well-structured policy framework can address these challenges by establishing clear guidelines for the collection, storage, and use of data, as well as setting standards for the ethical deployment of AI in IoT systems.

Moreover, policy frameworks are crucial for fostering innovation while ensuring that the risks associated with AI-IoT integration are mitigated. They can help balance the need for technological advancement with the protection of individual rights and societal interests. There might be a need to redefine the rights and societal interests in the new realm. By providing a structured approach to managing the complexities of AI-IoT integration, policymakers can create an environment that encourages responsible innovation, ensuring that the benefits of these technologies are widely shared while minimizing potential harms.

In addition, policy frameworks can facilitate interoperability and standardization across different AI-IoT systems, promoting a seamless integration of technologies on a global scale. This is particularly important as AI-IoT systems often operate across borders, requiring international cooperation and harmonization of regulations. A well-designed policy framework can help align different regulatory approaches, ensuring that AI-IoT systems can function effectively and securely in diverse environments.

The necessity of policy frameworks in AI-IoT integration extends to addressing the societal and economic impacts of these technologies. Policies can guide the development of AI-IoT systems in ways that promote economic growth and empowerment, societal relevance, and social inclusion, while also addressing potential negative impacts such as job displacement or increased inequality. By anticipating and addressing these issues through thoughtful policy design, policymakers can help ensure that the integration of AI and IoT contributes to a more equitable and sustainable future.

Technological Convergence of AI and IoT; Enhancing IoT with AI

The technological convergence of AI and IoT represents a significant shift in how we interact with technology, enabling unprecedented levels of automation, efficiency, and innovation. As AI systems gain the ability to process and analyze vast amounts of data generated by IoT devices, the integration of these technologies allows for smarter, more responsive environments. This convergence enables real-time decision-making, predictive analytics, and adaptive systems that can learn and evolve over time.

The enhancement of IoT with AI is a pivotal development in the digital age, where interconnected devices generate massive amounts of data that need intelligent processing to unlock their full potential. By integrating AI, IoT systems become more than just data collectors; they transform into smart systems capable of analyzing, learning, and making decisions autonomously. AI algorithms process data from IoT devices to derive insights, predict outcomes, and optimize operations across various sectors, thus generating "intelligence".

The integration of AI into IoT systems also presents challenges. The complexity of managing vast networks of intelligent devices requires robust frameworks for data security, privacy, and ethical AI deployment. As AI algorithms increasingly make decisions on behalf of users, ensuring transparency and accountability in these systems is crucial.

AI Enables Real-time Data Analysis, Predictive Analytics, and Autonomous Decision-making.

One of the main benefits of AI for IoT is real-time data analysis. IoT devices collect large volumes of data from various sources, such as sensors, cameras, or microphones. However, sending this data to a centralized cloud server for processing can be costly, time-consuming, and prone to latency and bandwidth issues. AI enables edge computing, where data is processed locally on the device or on a nearby node, reducing the need for data transmission and enabling faster and more efficient analysis. This allows IoT systems to respond in real time to changing conditions, events, or anomalies, and provide immediate feedback or actions.

Another benefit of AI for IoT is predictive analytics, where AI algorithms use historical and current data to forecast future outcomes or trends. Predictive analytics can help IoT systems optimize performance, prevent failures, and enhance user experience. For example, AI can analyze data from smart meters to predict energy demand and supply, and adjust the grid accordingly. AI can also monitor data from industrial equipment to detect signs of wear and tear, and schedule maintenance before breakdowns occur. AI can even analyze data from wearable devices to predict health risks and suggest preventive measures.

A third benefit of AI for IoT is autonomous decision-making, where AI algorithms can make decisions without human intervention, based on predefined rules or objectives. Autonomous decision-making can improve the efficiency, reliability, and safety of IoT systems, especially in complex or hazardous environments. For example, AI can enable autonomous vehicles to navigate traffic and avoid collisions, or drones to perform surveillance and delivery tasks. AI can also enable smart home systems to adjust lighting, temperature, and security settings according to user preferences and habits. AI can even enable smart farming systems to optimize irrigation, fertilization, and harvesting based on weather and soil conditions.

AI enables IoT systems to go beyond mere data collection and transmission, and become intelligent systems that can analyze, learn, and act on their own. By combining AI and IoT, we can create smart solutions that can improve various aspects of our lives, from energy and transportation, to health and agriculture. AI and IoT are two powerful technologies that can complement and enhance each other, and together, they can shape the future of the digital age.

Sectors Impacted by AI-IoT Integration

AI-IoT integration has a profound impact on multiple sectors, revolutionizing their operations and opening new possibilities for innovation and efficiency. Here are some key sectors that are significantly impacted:

1. Healthcare:

AI and IoT integration in healthcare enable remote patient monitoring, predictive diagnostics, and personalized treatments. Smart wearable devices collect real-time health data, while AI algorithms analyze this information to provide early warnings, detect anomalies, and even predict potential health risks before they escalate. This shift towards AI-driven IoT solutions improves patient care, reduces hospital readmissions, and optimizes healthcare resource utilization.

2. Manufacturing (Industry 4.0):

The manufacturing sector benefits greatly from AI-IoT integration, especially through predictive maintenance, process automation, and real-time supply chain monitoring. AI algorithms analyze IoT data from machinery and equipment to predict failures, optimize performance, and reduce downtime. This leads to improved operational efficiency, cost savings, and higher production quality.

3. Smart Cities:

In urban development, AI and IoT create smart cities by optimizing energy use, managing traffic flows, and enhancing public safety. Sensors embedded in infrastructure collect real-time data on everything from energy consumption to traffic congestion, which AI then analyzes to provide actionable insights. This enables efficient management of resources, reduces carbon footprints, and improves the quality of life for residents.

4. Agriculture:

Precision agriculture is revolutionized by AI-IoT integration, where sensors gather data on soil conditions, weather patterns, and crop health. AI processes this data to optimize irrigation, planting, and harvesting schedules. This leads to higher yields, reduced resource consumption, and more sustainable farming practices.

5. Transportation and Logistics:

The transportation and logistics sector is seeing significant improvements through AI-driven IoT. AI analyzes real-time data from IoT-enabled vehicles and transport systems, optimizing routes, predicting maintenance needs, and improving fuel efficiency. In logistics, this integration enables real-time tracking of goods, inventory management, and demand forecasting, streamlining operations across the supply chain.

6. Energy:

The energy sector benefits from AI-IoT by optimizing grid management, reducing energy waste, and integrating renewable energy sources. Smart meters and sensors provide data on energy usage, which AI algorithms analyze to forecast demand, reduce consumption during peak hours, and balance loads on the grid. AI also enables predictive maintenance of energy infrastructure.

7. Retail:

In retail, AI-IoT integration enhances customer experience, inventory management, and supply chain operations. Smart shelves, IoT sensors, and AI-powered analytics help retailers track inventory in real-time, optimize stock levels, and personalize customer experiences through data-driven insights.

8. Automotive:

Autonomous vehicles are perhaps the most visible example of AI-IoT integration. IoT sensors collect vast amounts of data from the vehicle's surroundings, while AI algorithms process this information to enable real-time decision-making, navigation, and collision avoidance. AI also enhances predictive maintenance and vehicle-to-vehicle communication.

9. Finance:

In finance, AI and IoT work together to streamline fraud detection, optimize investment strategies, and enhance customer services. IoT devices such as smart wallets, wearables, and biometric systems generate valuable data, which AI processes to improve financial forecasting, risk management, and personalized services for customers.

10. Telecommunications:

In telecommunications, AI-IoT integration enables more efficient network management, enhanced customer service, and smarter infrastructure. AI analyzes data from IoT-connected devices to predict network congestion, optimize bandwidth usage, and ensure seamless connectivity. Telecom providers also use AI-driven chatbots and virtual assistants to offer personalized support to customers based on real-time data from IoT devices.

11. Education:

AI and IoT are revolutionizing education by creating smart learning environments that are adaptive and personalized. IoT devices collect data on student engagement and learning patterns, while AI systems analyze this data to provide tailored learning experiences. From smart classrooms that adjust to students' needs to AI-driven educational platforms, this integration fosters more effective and individualized learning paths.

12. Home Automation:

The smart home sector benefits tremendously from AI-IoT integration. Devices like smart thermostats, lights, security systems, and appliances are interconnected through IoT, while AI algorithms automate and optimize their operations. This improves energy efficiency, enhances security, and provides greater convenience for homeowners through features like voice-activated controls and personalized settings based on behavioral data.

13. Environmental Monitoring:

AI-IoT integration plays a crucial role in monitoring and protecting the environment. IoT sensors collect data on air quality, water levels, and weather conditions, which AI systems analyze to predict natural disasters, optimize resource management, and track environmental changes. This convergence allows for real-time monitoring and more effective responses to climate change, pollution, and resource depletion.

14. Public Safety and Security:

AI-powered IoT systems are transforming public safety by enhancing surveillance, emergency response, and threat detection. Cameras, drones, and sensors gather real-time data, which AI algorithms analyze to detect potential security threats, improve crowd control, and aid in disaster management. AI's ability to analyze large datasets in real time allows for quicker and more efficient responses in emergency situations.

15. Hospitality:

In the hospitality industry, AI-IoT integration improves customer experiences through personalized services. Hotels and resorts use IoT devices to track guest preferences and comfort levels, while AI systems analyze this data to offer tailored recommendations, automate room settings, and enhance overall service quality. AI-driven chatbots also enhance customer service by responding to guest inquiries in real time.

16. Real Estate and Property Management:

The integration of AI and IoT is changing the way real estate is managed and sold. Smart buildings equipped with IoT sensors monitor energy usage, maintenance needs, and tenant behavior. AI systems use this data to optimize building operations, predict maintenance issues, and even enhance property security and value. Additionally, AI-IoT platforms help real estate professionals analyze market trends and make more informed decisions regarding property investments.

17. Defense and Military:

AI-IoT is also making a significant impact on defense and military operations. IoT devices in defense collect vast amounts of data from vehicles, equipment, and personnel, while AI systems analyze this information to enhance situational awareness, automate logistics, and support real-time decision-making on the battlefield. AI also enables predictive maintenance for military equipment, improving operational readiness.

18. Utilities:

In the utilities sector, AI and IoT work together to optimize the management of water, electricity, and gas systems. Smart meters and sensors monitor consumption patterns, while AI algorithms analyze this data to predict demand, prevent outages, and reduce waste. This results in more sustainable and efficient resource management, benefiting both providers and consumers.

19. Entertainment and Media:

AI and IoT are transforming the entertainment and media industry by personalizing content delivery and enhancing audience engagement. IoT-enabled devices collect user data, which AI systems analyze to recommend content based on viewing preferences and behaviors. This integration is also seen in smart TVs, gaming consoles, and streaming platforms, which offer personalized entertainment experiences driven by real-time data analysis.

20. Insurance:

The insurance sector is leveraging AI-IoT integration to offer more personalized policies and risk assessments.

IoT devices such as wearables and telematics in vehicles collect data on user behavior, while AI processes this data to calculate premiums, detect fraud, and predict risks. This not only improves customer satisfaction through tailored insurance products but also enhances operational efficiency for insurers.

The convergence of AI and IoT is transforming a wide range of sectors, bringing about new efficiencies, enhanced decision-making, and personalized experiences. However, as this integration grows, it requires robust policy frameworks to address concerns related to data privacy, security, and ethical considerations. The future impact of AI-IoT integration will be shaped not only by technological advancements but also by the regulatory and governance structures put in place to manage it responsibly.

Policy Challenges in AI-IoT Integration

The integration of AI and IoT presents complex policy challenges that span privacy, security, data ownership, and ethical considerations. With IoT devices generating massive amounts of data, there are significant privacy risks as AI algorithms use this data to enhance functionality. Policies must ensure a balance between innovation and privacy protection, creating a need for regulations that safeguard sensitive information. Additionally, the combination of AI and IoT heightens security concerns, particularly the risk of cyber-attacks. As a result, strict security protocols must be incorporated into policy frameworks to mitigate these threats.

A major obstacle to AI-IoT integration is the lack of standardized communication protocols. The fragmented ecosystem of devices and platforms across different manufacturers can limit the potential for seamless integration, thus requiring global interoperability standards. Without these standards, AI-IoT systems may not be able to communicate efficiently, hindering their effectiveness and deployment on a large scale. Policymakers must address this by encouraging global cooperation to develop and implement these standards.

At the same time, regulatory frameworks must be developed to oversee AI-IoT applications. Many countries currently lack clear guidelines on emerging technologies, and policymakers must strike a balance between fostering innovation and addressing potential risks. These frameworks need to be flexible and adaptable to the fast-evolving nature of AI and IoT while establishing clear accountability in cases where AI-driven systems malfunction or cause harm. Furthermore, transparency and fairness in AI's decision-making processes are critical ethical concerns that need to be regulated, ensuring equitable use of AI-IoT technologies.

Data sovereignty and cross-border data flows present additional challenges, particularly as IoT devices frequently transfer data across regions with varying data protection regulations. Policymakers must develop solutions that enable the smooth exchange of data without undermining national data sovereignty. Public trust in AI-IoT systems also needs to be fostered through transparent policies and public education efforts to close the gap between technological advancement and societal acceptance. The digital divide, particularly in regions with limited infrastructure, needs attention to ensure equitable access to AI-IoT benefits across different geographies.

Sustainability is another growing concern, as the power consumption of AI and IoT devices is substantial. This necessitates policies promoting energy-efficient designs and the use of renewable energy sources to mitigate the environmental impact of widespread AI-IoT adoption. The role of blockchain in AI-IoT integration provides a promising solution for secure, transparent data exchanges, particularly in sectors requiring high data integrity like healthcare and finance. Policymakers should consider leveraging blockchain to build trust in AI-IoT ecosystems by establishing secure, tamper-proof data-sharing mechanisms.

Moreover, the transition from IPv4 to IPv6 is crucial for the growth of AI-IoT ecosystems. IPv4's limited address space is insufficient to support the ever-growing number of connected devices, while IPv6 offers a far greater number of IP addresses. However, the transition to IPv6 is happening unevenly across regions, with countries like China leading in its adoption, while the U.S. and Europe lag behind. Global standardization of IPv6 is essential for ensuring that AI-IoT devices can communicate effectively across borders and platforms.

The geopolitical landscape also complicates the standardization process, with countries like the U.S., China, and the EU competing for technological dominance. This competition influences global standard-setting, creating challenges in achieving cohesive global policies. To navigate these complexities, public-private partnerships will be crucial in developing innovative solutions and infrastructures that support AI-IoT ecosystems. These collaborations, along with public education programs, can also help prepare the workforce for an increasingly automated world.

The integration of AI and IoT requires forward-thinking policy frameworks that address a range of challenges, from privacy and security to global standardization and sustainability. Policymakers, industry leaders, and civil society must collaborate to ensure the responsible and beneficial deployment of AI-IoT technologies across sectors.

The Liability and Accountability: Legal implications and accountability in cases of AI-IoT system failures:

Liability and accountability are critical legal concerns when it comes to AI-IoT system failures. Determining who is responsible when these systems malfunction—whether it's the device manufacturer, the AI algorithm developer, the IoT service provider, the connectivity provider, or even the end-user—poses a significant challenge. This complexity often results from the multi-layered nature of AI-IoT systems, which involve interconnected devices, networks, and algorithms, each potentially developed by different entities.

Legal frameworks must clearly outline the allocation of liability in cases where AI-IoT systems cause harm or fail to perform as expected. For example, in autonomous vehicles, where AI algorithms and IoT sensors drive decision-making, the question arises: is the car manufacturer responsible for accidents, or is it the software developer that programmed the AI? Similarly, in healthcare, if a smart medical device fails, who is held accountable—the device manufacturer, the data provider, or the AI system designer?

In addition, the lack of clear legal precedents and guidelines makes it challenging for courts to adjudicate disputes arising from AI-IoT failures. Policymakers need to develop flexible but robust legal frameworks that cover different aspects of AI-IoT integration, such as system transparency, accountability mechanisms, and risk assessments.

Accountability also plays a major role, as the opacity of AI decision-making processes (sometimes referred to as the "black box" problem) can make it difficult to trace failures back to a specific cause. Legal systems must therefore require that AI-IoT technologies are designed with transparency and auditability in mind, ensuring that failures can be investigated thoroughly and responsibilities assigned appropriately.

In sum, policymakers must work to establish legal clarity surrounding liability and accountability in AI-IoT integration to protect consumers and ensure the responsible development of these technologies. Beyond just assigning responsibility for failures, a system needs to be developed that can learn from its actions and incorporate historical data, effectively creating a feedback loop that allows AI-IoT systems to improve over time. This includes the use of previous precedents—both actions and inactions—to guide decision-making, helping these systems evolve in a way that prevents future failures. Such an adaptive approach would not only enhance accountability but also ensure more resilient, intelligent, and self-correcting systems. This would mitigate risks and enable more trustworthy deployment of AI-IoT technologies across industries.

Impact on Employment and Society - Societal shifts due to AI-IoT integration, including job displacement and the digital divide.

The integration of AI and IoT is expected to bring profound societal shifts, with both positive and negative consequences. One major concern is job displacement, as automation powered by AI-IoT systems could replace many roles in sectors like manufacturing, logistics, and retail. Routine, manual, and repetitive tasks are particularly at risk, as these systems can often perform them more efficiently. However, while some jobs will be lost, AI-IoT integration will also create new roles, especially in areas requiring advanced skills, such as AI development, IoT management, and data science. To mitigate the negative impact, governments and organizations must invest in retraining programs and educational initiatives to equip the workforce with the skills needed for these emerging opportunities.

Moreover, the digital divide may widen as the benefits of AI-IoT integration disproportionately favor those with access to advanced technology and high-speed internet. Urban and developed areas are more likely to benefit from AI-IoT innovations in sectors like healthcare, education, and transportation, leaving rural and underserved communities behind. To address this, policymakers must focus on ensuring equitable access to the infrastructure that supports AI-IoT, such as reliable internet connectivity and affordable smart devices. Bridging this gap will be crucial in ensuring that AI-IoT technologies contribute to societal progress for all, rather than deepening existing inequalities.

Adaptive Regulatory Frameworks for AI-IoT

As the integration of Artificial Intelligence (AI) and the Internet of Things (IoT) continues to transform industries and societies, the need for adaptive regulatory frameworks becomes increasingly critical. These frameworks aim to address the unique challenges and opportunities presented by AI-IoT technologies, ensuring their safe, ethical, and effective deployment across various sectors.

Designing effective policy frameworks for AI-IoT integration requires a multi-dimensional approach that addresses the technological, legal, ethical, and socio-economic implications of these converging technologies. First and foremost, policies must focus on data privacy and security, given the vast amounts of personal and sensitive information collected by IoT devices and analyzed by AI algorithms. Ensuring that this data is adequately protected through strict regulations like GDPR, alongside new standards for consent, encryption, and data minimization, will be essential.

Second, standardization and interoperability must be a priority. The global nature of AI-IoT ecosystems requires that devices, platforms, and systems from different manufacturers and regions can seamlessly communicate with each other. Establishing international standards for communication protocols, data formats, and security practices will facilitate smoother integration and encourage innovation across borders.

Another key aspect is addressing legal liability and accountability in cases where AI-IoT systems fail or cause harm. Clear guidelines must be established to determine who is responsible in such situations—whether it is the AI developer, the IoT device manufacturer, or the service provider. Additionally, regulations should define accountability mechanisms for autonomous decision-making systems, particularly when these systems have significant real-world impacts, such as in healthcare or autonomous vehicles.

Ethical considerations must also be a central part of policy design. Issues like algorithmic bias, transparency in decision-making, and the ethical use of data need to be addressed to ensure that AI-IoT technologies are deployed in a manner that is fair and just. Policymakers must enforce ethical AI practices and ensure that consent for data collection and usage is transparent, especially in consumer applications.

Furthermore, policy frameworks should encourage public-private partnerships to foster innovation while safeguarding public interests. Collaborations between governments, tech companies, and academic institutions can help advance AI-IoT integration while ensuring compliance with societal norms and legal requirements. Regulatory sandboxes—controlled environments for testing new technologies—could be a useful tool for balancing innovation with regulation.

Lastly, inclusivity and digital equity must be emphasized. As AI-IoT integration progresses, policies should aim to bridge the digital divide by promoting access to necessary infrastructure, such as affordable internet and smart devices, especially in rural and underserved areas. This will help ensure that the benefits of AI-IoT are distributed equitably across society, minimizing the risk of further exacerbating socio-economic inequalities.

The policy design for AI-IoT integration must be holistic, adaptive, and forward-looking. It should address the immediate challenges while remaining flexible enough to evolve with technological advancements, ensuring that AI-IoT systems are deployed in a manner that benefits society at large while minimizing risks.

Core Components of Adaptive Regulatory Frameworks

Technological Development

Adaptive regulatory frameworks must acknowledge the varying levels of technological development between regions. Developed countries, with their established infrastructures and legal systems, focus on refining and enhancing these structures. Conversely, developing countries are tasked with building foundational systems from the ground up, necessitating a flexible approach to regulation that allows for incremental advancements.

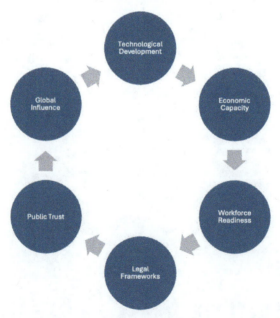

Economic Capacity

Wealthier nations possess the financial resources to invest heavily in research and development (R&D), infrastructure upgrades, and leadership in global standards. Developing countries, however, may depend on international assistance and a phased approach to technology adoption. Regulatory frameworks must therefore be tailored to accommodate these economic disparities, promoting equitable access to AI-IoT benefits.

Workforce Readiness

The readiness of the workforce is a crucial factor in the adoption of AI-IoT technologies. Developed countries, with their higher skill levels and advanced education systems, can implement these technologies more rapidly. In contrast, developing countries face challenges related to reskilling and digital literacy. Adaptive frameworks should include provisions for education and training programs to bridge this gap.

Legal Frameworks

Developed nations often have comprehensive data privacy and cybersecurity regulations in place, providing a robust foundation for AI-IoT integration. Developing countries, on the other hand, may need to draft new regulations that address the unique risks and benefits of these technologies. Adaptive regulatory frameworks should facilitate the development of these legal structures in a manner that is both timely and context-specific.

Public Trust

Public trust is a significant determinant of the success of AI-IoT initiatives. In developed countries, there is a heightened emphasis on consumer protection and ethical AI practices. Developing nations, meanwhile, are focused on building broader awareness and establishing trust within their populations. Regulatory frameworks should thus incorporate strategies for transparency, accountability, and public engagement.

Global Influence

Developed countries often play a pivotal role in setting international standards for AI-IoT technologies. Developing countries, in turn, focus on adopting these standards to integrate seamlessly into the global market. Adaptive frameworks should promote international collaboration and the sharing of best practices to ensure harmonized progress worldwide.

The key policy requirements for developing countries and developed countries in AI-IoT integration, along with the factors that contribute to differences in policy styles and governance:

Policy Area	Developing Countries	Developed Countries	Contributing Factors
Infrastructure Development	Focus on building foundational infrastructure, such as internet access, power supply, and affordable IoT devices.	Prioritize upgrading and maintaining high-speed, advanced infrastructure for AI-IoT systems.	Level of technological advancement, access to capital, existing infrastructure gaps.
Digital Divide	Policies to promote digital literacy, access to affordable devices, and internet for underserved populations.	Policies may focus on inclusion for marginalized groups, but more resources are allocated for cutting-edge innovations.	Economic development levels, inequality in access to technology and education.

Policy Area	Developing Countries	Developed Countries	Contributing Factors
Data Privacy & Security	Policies may need to prioritize basic data protection laws, particularly as digital transformation accelerates.	Advanced and stringent data protection laws like GDPR or CCPA are already in place. Focus on enforcing and updating them.	Maturity of existing legal frameworks, levels of digital literacy among the population.
Regulation & Compliance	Development of initial regulatory frameworks for AI-IoT, with flexibility to adapt to rapid change. International collaboration might be necessary to adopt global standards.	Regulatory frameworks are well established but need constant updating. Focus is on refining existing laws and ensuring compliance with international standards.	Legal maturity, capacity for enforcement, degree of international collaboration.
Standardization & Interoperability	Focus on adopting international standards and avoiding fragmentation in IoT and AI ecosystems.	Focus on developing and leading global standards in collaboration with key international stakeholders.	Role in global technology leadership, influence over international standards bodies.
Cybersecurity	Emphasis on building basic cybersecurity infrastructure and protecting critical systems from threats.	Focus on advanced cybersecurity measures, with policies aimed at safeguarding critical infrastructure and mitigating sophisticated threats.	Level of cyber threats, maturity of tech infrastructure, availability of cybersecurity expertise.

Policy Area	Developing Countries	Developed Countries	Contributing Factors
Workforce Development & Job Displacement	Policies focused on reskilling and upskilling workers in sectors impacted by automation. Government-led initiatives for training the workforce to embrace digital economies.	Greater emphasis on innovation and high-tech job creation. Policies aim at managing job displacement through advanced retraining programs.	Existing workforce skill levels, capacity for large-scale training programs, economic transition.
Ethical Governance	Developing frameworks to ensure ethical AI use, prevent bias, and promote transparency in decision-making.	More mature frameworks already in place, with an emphasis on refining ethical AI and ensuring accountability in complex use cases.	Degree of AI integration in society, legal capacity for ethical enforcement, public trust in institutions.
Sustainability & Energy Consumption	Policies will focus on energy-efficient AI-IoT technologies, balancing development with sustainability goals.	Focus on stringent sustainability standards, incentivizing renewable energy use in AI-IoT infrastructure.	Energy access, environmental concerns, commitment to international climate agreements.
Public-Private Partnerships	Governments may need external funding and expertise from international organizations or private sectors for AI-IoT implementation.	Strong emphasis on fostering domestic innovation through partnerships with tech companies and research institutions.	Access to private capital, technological development, reliance on foreign expertise.

Policy Area	Developing Countries	Developed Countries	Contributing Factors
Cross-Border Data Flows & Sovereignty	Policies will likely prioritize national sovereignty over data, balancing global collaboration with protectionism.	Focus on balancing global data exchange with robust local data protection laws. Likely participation in multilateral agreements for data governance.	Geopolitical positioning, role in international trade, technological dependencies.
Trust & Public Perception	Policies should focus on building trust in AI-IoT systems, educating the population on their benefits and potential risks.	Policies already address public trust but continue to evolve as AI-IoT becomes more pervasive. Focus on transparency and consumer protection.	Level of public trust in technology, past experiences with tech adoption, media influence.

The above table provides a comparison between the different focuses of AI-IoT policy development in developing and developed countries, shaped by their unique socio-economic, technological, and regulatory environments.

Key Factors Influencing Different Policy Styles:

1. **Technological Development:** Developed countries generally have the infrastructure and legal frameworks in place, while developing countries are building foundational systems.

2. **Economic Capacity:** Wealthier nations can invest more in advanced R&D, infrastructure upgrades, and global standards leadership, while developing countries may rely more on international assistance and gradual technology adoption.

3. **Workforce Readiness:** The skill levels in developed countries may enable quicker adoption of AI-IoT, while developing countries may face challenges with reskilling and digital literacy.

4. **Legal Frameworks:** Developed countries often have stringent data privacy and cybersecurity laws, whereas developing countries may need to draft new regulations in response to emerging technologies.

5. **Public Trust:** Developed countries tend to focus more on consumer protection and ethical AI, while developing countries are working on creating broader awareness and building trust.

6. **Global Influence:** Developed nations often set international standards, while developing nations may focus on adopting these standards to integrate into the global market.

Collaborative Governance Models

The dynamic nature of AI-IoT technologies necessitates a collaborative approach to governance. This involves stakeholders from government, industry, academia, and civil society working together to create regulations that are both effective and flexible. Collaborative governance models can help ensure that regulatory frameworks remain responsive to technological advancements and societal needs.

Adaptive regulatory frameworks for AI-IoT are essential for fostering innovation while safeguarding public interests. By considering factors such as technological development, economic capacity, workforce readiness, legal frameworks, public trust, and global influence, these frameworks can be tailored to meet the diverse needs of different regions. Through collaborative governance, we can achieve a balanced approach that maximizes the benefits of AI-IoT technologies for all.

The Need for Policies that Evolve Alongside Technological Advancements

The rapid development of the emerging technologies including, AI and IoT technologies highlights the critical need for policies that evolve in tandem with technological advancements. These technologies are progressing at an unprecedented rate, presenting both opportunities and challenges that require adaptive governance. Static policies, while useful for addressing immediate concerns, often fall short as technological capabilities and their associated risks expand. Therefore, creating a flexible policy framework that can keep pace with innovations is essential.

One of the key reasons for evolving policies is the dynamic nature of AI and IoT. As these technologies continue to advance, new challenges emerge, particularly in areas like cybersecurity, privacy, and data ethics. For instance, as IoT devices become more interconnected, they increase the risk of cyberattacks, necessitating continuously updated security protocols. Policies that can adapt to such rapid changes ensure that governments and organizations are better equipped to manage emerging threats.

In addition, evolving policies are crucial for addressing the global interoperability of AI-IoT systems. Without standardized frameworks, different regions and manufacturers may develop fragmented ecosystems, limiting the potential of these technologies. Policymakers must continuously refine and realign international standards that promote seamless integration and cooperation across borders, fostering innovation and economic growth.

Balancing innovation with consumer protection is another core reason why policies must evolve. AI and IoT offer immense potential for enhancing business operations, healthcare, and public services, but unchecked innovation can lead to serious risks. Evolving policies can maintain this balance by allowing technological progress while implementing safeguards to protect privacy, security, and ethical standards.

Liability and accountability are also growing concerns as AI and IoT systems become more autonomous, while creating new norms. With machines making decisions with less human oversight, policymakers must establish clear guidelines on accountability when these systems fail or cause harm. Evolving policies ensure that legal frameworks keep up with increasingly complex and independent systems, offering clarity on who is responsible when things go wrong.

Additionally, ethical considerations, particularly concerning bias and transparency in AI systems, require policies that are responsive to technological advancements. As machine learning models become more sophisticated, they have the potential to perpetuate biases or make decisions that are difficult to interpret. Policies that evolve to address these concerns can help ensure that AI remains fair and transparent. It is important to understand that the nature of biases will also be evolving and keeping a transparent mechanisms might get complicated over time. So such provisions needs to be imagined or kept in mind for flexibility.

Environmental sustainability is another critical area where evolving policies are necessary. The energy demands of AI and IoT systems are growing, contributing to significant environmental impacts. Policies promoting energy-efficient designs and the use of renewable energy are essential for ensuring that technological advancements do not come at the cost of the planet.

Finally, the global competition for AI and IoT dominance adds another layer of complexity. Countries that fail to develop or update their policies in response to international competition may fall behind in the race for technological leadership. Evolving policies ensure that nations remain competitive while also fostering cooperation on global standards.

The fast-paced evolution of AI and IoT technologies requires equally dynamic policy frameworks. By adapting to the latest advancements and anticipating future challenges, governments and organizations can ensure that these technologies are deployed responsibly and sustainably, balancing innovation with protection and ethics.

Examples of Adaptive Regulation in Other Domains

Adaptive regulation has proven to be a valuable approach in several fast-evolving sectors, where rigid regulatory frameworks may stifle innovation or fail to address new risks. By allowing laws and guidelines to evolve in tandem with technological advancements or emerging challenges, adaptive regulation helps ensure that governance keeps pace with progress while maintaining public safety, ethical standards, and market fairness.

1. Financial Technology (FinTech)

One of the most prominent examples of adaptive regulation can be seen in the FinTech sector, where innovations such as digital banking, blockchain, and cryptocurrencies have transformed traditional financial systems. The introduction of regulatory sandboxes in many countries exemplifies adaptive regulation at its core. These sandboxes create controlled environments where startups and established financial institutions can test new financial products, services, or business models under relaxed regulatory oversight.

The purpose of such an approach is twofold: first, it allows innovators to develop and trial cutting-edge financial technologies without the constraints of fully formed regulatory frameworks, which might otherwise slow down their progress. Second, it provides regulators with real-world data on how these innovations function in practice, helping to shape future laws and standards. For example, the UK's Financial Conduct Authority (FCA) and similar regulatory bodies in countries like Singapore and Australia have led the charge by allowing companies to experiment with blockchain-based financial products, digital lending platforms, and mobile banking solutions. The insights gained from these sandboxes inform broader regulatory reforms and help develop more effective, future-proof financial regulations.

2. Healthcare and Medical Innovation

In the field of healthcare, particularly with pharmaceuticals and medical devices, adaptive regulatory approaches have become critical in responding to urgent public health needs. Traditionally, drug development and approval processes could take years, but in certain cases, especially in life-threatening or rare conditions, this timeline becomes untenable. To address this, agencies such as the U.S. Food and Drug Administration (FDA) and the European Medicines Agency (EMA) have developed accelerated approval pathways, including the Breakthrough Therapy Designation and Fast Track approvals.

These regulatory pathways allow companies developing promising therapies for critical diseases to speed up the approval process based on preliminary clinical evidence.

For example, in the fight against diseases like cancer or rare genetic disorders, adaptive frameworks have enabled drugs to reach the market much more quickly while allowing regulators to gather post-market data and adjust their oversight accordingly. Similarly, the approval process for COVID-19 vaccines showcased a global shift towards adaptive regulation, where emergency use authorizations allowed for rapid deployment without compromising public safety. This dynamic approach balances the urgency of public health crises with the need for ongoing safety monitoring and risk assessment.

3. Environmental Regulation and Sustainability

In response to the global challenge of climate change, governments have increasingly turned to adaptive regulatory systems in the environmental sector. For instance, cap-and-trade systems for carbon emissions are a prime example of adaptive governance in practice. Under these systems, governments set an overall cap on the amount of greenhouse gases that industries can emit. Companies are then issued emissions permits or credits, which they can trade with one another depending on their own carbon footprint.

This market-based approach provides flexibility by allowing companies to find cost-effective ways to reduce emissions. The cap itself is adaptable and can be tightened over time, based on environmental targets or new technological capabilities. The European Union Emissions Trading System (EU ETS), one of the largest carbon markets globally, illustrates this model. It started with relatively modest caps to encourage participation, but over the years, it has progressively lowered allowable emissions to push industries toward cleaner technologies. Adaptive regulation in this context ensures that environmental goals are met without causing undue economic disruption, allowing the system to evolve as needed.

4. Autonomous Vehicles (AVs)

The development of autonomous vehicles (AVs) represents another sector where adaptive regulation is essential due to the fast-paced advancements in AI-driven mobility. Governments and transportation regulators face the challenge of striking a balance between promoting innovation and ensuring public safety as AVs become more common on public roads. In the United States, the National Highway Traffic Safety Administration (NHTSA) has developed iterative guidelines for autonomous vehicle testing. Rather than rigid laws, the guidelines are updated regularly as the technology matures and new safety data becomes available.

This adaptive approach allows manufacturers to test AVs in real-world conditions while giving regulators time to develop safety standards based on evolving information. Moreover, AV regulation often varies by state in the U.S., with states like California and Arizona adopting different degrees of permissiveness. This flexibility in governance ensures that innovation is not stifled while maintaining a level of caution. Adaptive regulatory frameworks in this domain also focus on liability questions—determining who is responsible in cases of accidents involving autonomous vehicles—while allowing for the incremental rollout of more advanced autonomous driving features.

5. Cybersecurity

In the digital age, cybersecurity has become a critical domain where adaptive regulation is necessary due to the ever-evolving nature of cyber threats. One significant example is the General Data Protection Regulation (GDPR) in the European Union. While GDPR provides a robust framework for data protection and privacy, it also includes mechanisms for updating security requirements as technology and threats evolve. Companies handling data must meet specific standards, but these standards can change over time to account for new risks or breakthroughs in cybersecurity measures.

Another adaptive regulatory approach in cybersecurity can be seen in the **U.S. National Institute of Standards and Technology (NIST)** Cybersecurity Framework, which is regularly updated with the latest best practices for securing systems against attacks. By keeping regulations adaptable, both companies and governments can respond more effectively to the fast-changing landscape of digital threats, minimizing damage while encouraging the adoption of new, more secure technologies.

In these domains—FinTech, healthcare, environmental regulation, autonomous vehicles, and cybersecurity— adaptive regulation has proven crucial for enabling innovation while safeguarding public interest and welfare. Each sector demonstrates the importance of creating regulatory frameworks that are flexible enough to evolve alongside technological progress. This approach ensures that governments and industries can respond to emerging risks, learn from ongoing developments, and refine regulations as new technologies disrupt traditional practices.

By adopting a mindset of flexibility and forward-thinking governance, adaptive regulation helps strike the necessary balance between fostering innovation and protecting society from unintended consequences, proving indispensable in a rapidly changing world.

Collaborative Governance Models

Collaborative governance models have emerged as vital frameworks for addressing the increasingly complex and interdisciplinary challenges posed by rapid technological advancements, particularly in sectors such as AI and IoT integration. Traditional regulatory approaches, often rooted in hierarchical structures and slower decision-making processes, struggle to keep up with the speed at which technology evolves. In contrast, collaborative governance embraces a more dynamic and inclusive method, leveraging the strengths of various stakeholders to create balanced, adaptive, and forward-thinking policy solutions. This approach involves ongoing dialogue, flexibility, and transparency, with all participants working towards shared objectives while balancing different interests.

SMART Policy Making: Multi-Stakeholder Collaboration Among Governments, Industry, and Civil Society (S.M.A.R.T: Sustainable Multi-stakeholder Adaptive Regulatory Transformation)

One of the core principles of SMART collaborative governance is the inclusion of diverse stakeholders in the policymaking process. Multi-stakeholder collaboration, which brings together governments, industry leaders, civil society, and sometimes academia, helps create a well-rounded approach to the regulation of emerging technologies. Each group plays a critical role in shaping policy: governments provide legal frameworks and public safety oversight, industry actors contribute technical expertise and market realities, and civil society ensures that the ethical, social, and equity concerns of the broader public are incorporated.

Figure B: SMART Policy Making

1. **Role of Governments:** Governments act as regulators and enforcers of laws that protect public interest, maintain national security, and ensure market stability. However, due to the technical complexity and novelty of technologies like AI and

IoT, regulators often require input from industry experts to grasp the full spectrum of technological implications. This partnership allows for better-informed regulations that align with technological realities while safeguarding public welfare. Governments can also act as conveners, bringing different stakeholders together to build consensus and establish unified policy goals.

2. **Industry Participation:** Companies and innovators in the technology sector drive the development and deployment of AI-IoT systems. These entities are often on the frontlines of understanding how these technologies function and what risks they may pose. Industry participants can provide critical feedback on how regulations might impact innovation and market competitiveness. Their involvement ensures that regulatory frameworks do not stifle innovation but instead promote responsible technological growth. Industry leaders often advocate for policies that allow for flexible experimentation, such as regulatory sandboxes, where innovations can be tested under a lighter regulatory touch before being scaled.

3. **Civil Society/Media's Contribution:** Civil society organizations (CSOs), including NGOs, consumer rights groups, media and ethical watchdogs, represent the concerns of individuals and communities who may be affected by AI-IoT deployment. These groups advocate for privacy rights, digital equity, data protection, and ethical considerations, ensuring that human rights and societal values are upheld. Their involvement is particularly crucial in addressing the unintended consequences of technological advancement, such as algorithmic bias, surveillance concerns, or the digital divide. By bringing these perspectives into

the policy conversation, CSOs/Media help ensure that AI and IoT technologies are developed and implemented in ways that are inclusive, equitable, and beneficial to all members of society.

Through multi-stakeholder collaboration, policymakers can balance technical feasibility, economic growth, and societal values, leading to more robust and sustainable policy outcomes. Initiatives like the Internet Governance Forum (IGF) or the Partnership on AI, which bring together representatives from governments, industry, and civil society to discuss and develop best practices for AI deployment, exemplify how multi-stakeholder governance can work in practice. This model fosters a continuous exchange of ideas and keeps policy frameworks up to date with the rapid pace of technological change.

Co-Creating Policies That Balance Innovation with Regulation

The co-creation of policies between stakeholders is essential for ensuring that regulations keep pace with technological developments without hindering innovation. In the AI-IoT space, where innovation is rapid and continuous, co-creation allows for more agile policy frameworks that can adapt to evolving technologies and emerging challenges. This process encourages proactive policymaking rather than reactive regulation, which often lags behind technological advancements.

1. **Regulatory Flexibility:** Co-creation involves an ongoing dialogue between regulators, industry experts, media and societal representatives, which allows for a more flexible approach to policy. Traditional regulation often faces the challenge of being too rigid, unable to adapt to the fast-evolving nature of technology. In contrast, co-created

policies are designed to be iterative, meaning they can be revised and updated as new technologies emerge or as unintended consequences become apparent. For example, in the field of autonomous vehicles, regulatory frameworks are being developed collaboratively by governments and automotive companies through pilot programs and test sites, ensuring that policies evolve as the technology advances.

2. **Regulatory Sandboxes:** One of the practical applications of co-created policies is the concept of regulatory sandboxes. These are controlled environments where companies can test their innovations under relaxed regulatory conditions, allowing them to explore the capabilities and risks of new technologies without facing full regulatory compliance from the outset. Sandboxes offer a space where industry and regulators can work together to understand how technologies perform in real-world conditions, while civil society can provide input on ethical, social, and legal implications. This collaborative approach encourages innovation while ensuring that regulators remain informed about technological progress and potential risks.

3. **Balancing Innovation and Public Safety:** The goal of co-creation is to strike a delicate balance between promoting innovation and protecting public safety and welfare. Overregulation, especially in its early stages, can stifle innovation by creating excessive barriers to entry or by limiting experimentation. Conversely, under-regulation can expose consumers to significant risks, such as data breaches, security vulnerabilities, or unethical practices. The co-creation process ensures that policies are both enabling and protective, allowing

for technological advancements while maintaining the necessary safeguards to protect individuals and society at large.

4. **Examples of Co-Created Policies:** A prime example of successful co-creation is the European Union's General Data Protection Regulation (GDPR). This landmark policy was developed through extensive consultation with industry, consumer rights groups, and civil society organizations to create a comprehensive framework for data protection that balances the need for innovation with stringent privacy safeguards. GDPR has set a global benchmark for data privacy and is an example of how collaborative governance can lead to influential, forward-thinking policy outcomes. Other co-created frameworks include initiatives in FinTech regulation, where financial authorities and startups collaborate to create adaptive frameworks for digital currencies and blockchain technologies.

5. **Sustainability and Ethical Concerns:** The co-creation process also plays a crucial role in addressing broader issues such as sustainability and ethics in AI-IoT governance. As AI and IoT systems expand, they contribute to growing energy consumption and raise questions about environmental impact. Moreover, ethical concerns such as algorithmic bias, transparency, and accountability need to be incorporated into governance models. Co-created policies ensure that all these considerations are integrated from the outset, creating a holistic approach that aligns innovation with ethical responsibility and environmental sustainability.

Long-Term Impact of Collaborative Governance and SMART Policy Making.

Collaborative governance or the SMART Policy making is not only about solving immediate regulatory challenges but also about establishing a long-term framework for continuous engagement among stakeholders. As technologies like AI and IoT continue to evolve, the need for adaptive, responsive, and inclusive governance will become more critical. By involving multiple stakeholders in the policymaking process, collaborative governance models help to future-proof regulatory frameworks, ensuring they can evolve alongside technological advancements. Moreover, by fostering trust between governments, industry, media and civil society, these models build a foundation for sustainable innovation that benefits all segments of society.

The collaborative governance models or SMART Policy design are essential for navigating the complexities of AI-IoT integration. By bringing together governments, industry, media and civil society in a co-creation process, these models ensure that policies are flexible, adaptive, and inclusive. They strike a balance between encouraging technological innovation and safeguarding public welfare, ultimately creating a regulatory environment that fosters responsible and sustainable growth.

Ethical AI Guidelines and Their Importance

Ethical AI Guidelines are sets of principles, policies, and frameworks that aim to ensure that artificial intelligence (AI) is developed, deployed, and used in a manner that is consistent with moral and ethical standards. As AI systems become more integrated into various sectors of society—from healthcare and finance to transportation and entertainment—the potential impact on individuals and communities grows. This makes the establishment of ethical AI guidelines a critical part of responsible technology governance. UNESCO has set a basic Ethical AI Guidelines: https://www.unesco.org/en/artificial-intelligence/recommendation-ethics[3]

The emergence of Artificial Intelligence (AI) has brought about transformative changes in society, presenting both significant opportunities and challenges. As AI systems increasingly influence various aspects of our lives, the need for ethical guidelines has become paramount. With its unique mandate, UNESCO has led the international effort to ensure that science and technology develop with strong ethical guardrails for decades. Be it on genetic research, climate change, or scientific research, UNESCO has delivered global standards to maximize the

---

3   Ethical AI Guidelines by UNESCO: https://www.unesco.org/en/artificial-intelligence/recommendation-ethics

benefits of the scientific discoveries, while minimizing the downside risks, ensuring they contribute to a more inclusive, sustainable, and peaceful world. It has also identified frontier challenges in areas such as the ethics of neurotechnology, on climate engineering, and the internet of things.

Recognizing this, the **Global AI Ethics and Governance Observatory** under UNESCO aims to provide essential resources for policymakers, regulators, academics, and civil society, facilitating a collaborative approach to addressing the pressing challenges posed by AI. The observatory serves as a global hub to assess countries' readiness to adopt AI ethically and responsibly while showcasing impactful research, toolkits, and good practices to inform AI governance.

The Ethical Compass in AI Development

The ethical compass is critically relevant in the realm of AI. As these technologies reshape how we work, interact, and live, they risk embedding biases, threatening human rights, and contributing to environmental degradation. The Recommendation on the Ethics of Artificial Intelligence[4], published by UNESCO in November 2021, serves as the first global standard on AI ethics, applicable to all member states. At its core, this recommendation emphasizes the protection of human rights and dignity, fostering a responsible approach to AI development that prioritizes transparency, fairness, and human oversight.

Core Values of the Recommendation

The recommendation outlines four foundational values essential for guiding AI systems toward serving humanity and the environment:

---

4   Recommendations on the Ethics of Artificial Intelligence: https://unesdoc.un-esco.org/ark:/48223/pf0000381137

1. **Human Rights and Human Dignity:** Emphasizes respect for and protection of fundamental freedoms.

2. **Peaceful and Just Societies:** Advocates for living in interconnected communities that prioritize justice.

3. **Diversity and Inclusiveness:** Promotes the inclusion of diverse perspectives and voices in AI development.

4. **Environmental and Ecosystem Flourishing:** Recognizes the importance of sustainable practices in AI deployment.

A Human Rights-Centered Approach

The Recommendation delineates ten core principles that embody a human rights-centered approach to AI ethics:

1. **Proportionality and Do No Harm:** AI use must be necessary and minimize potential harm.

2. **Safety and Security:** AI systems should mitigate both safety and security risks.

3. **Right to Privacy and Data Protection:** Safeguarding privacy is crucial throughout the AI lifecycle.

4. **Multi-Stakeholder Governance:** Diverse stakeholder participation is essential for inclusive AI governance.

5. **Responsibility and Accountability:** AI systems must be auditable and traceable, with mechanisms in place for accountability.

6. **Transparency and Explainability:** AI systems should be transparent, ensuring users understand their functioning.

7. **Human Oversight and Determination:** Human responsibility should remain paramount in AI decision-making.

8. **Sustainability:** AI technologies should be evaluated against their sustainability impacts.

9. **Awareness and Literacy:** Promoting public understanding of AI is vital for informed engagement.

10. **Fairness and Non-Discrimination:** AI development must ensure social justice and equitable access to benefits.

Actionable Policies for Implementation

While ethical principles form the foundation of AI governance, practical strategies are necessary to ensure effective implementation. The Recommendation outlines eleven key policy areas where member states can focus efforts to develop responsible AI practices. These areas include data governance, education, environmental considerations, and health and social well-being.

UNESCO has also developed two methodologies to aid member states in implementing these guidelines:

- **Readiness Assessment Methodology (RAM):** This tool assesses a country's preparedness to adopt the ethical standards outlined in the Recommendation.
- **Ethical Impact Assessment (EIA):** EIA enables AI project teams to evaluate potential impacts and devise harm prevention strategies in collaboration with affected communities.

Women4Ethical AI Initiative

To further promote gender equality in AI, UNESCO's Women4Ethical AI platform unites leading female experts across various sectors. The initiative aims to ensure that women's perspectives are integral to the design and deployment of AI systems, while also advocating for non-discriminatory algorithms and data sources.

Business Council for Ethics of AI

In partnership with private sector entities in Latin America, the Business Council for Ethics of AI serves as a collaborative platform for companies to share experiences and advance ethical practices within the AI industry. Co-chaired by Microsoft and Telefonica, this council emphasizes building technical capacities in ethics and AI, developing tools like the Ethical Impact Assessment, and contributing to regional regulatory frameworks that uphold human rights and ethical standards.

The establishment of ethical guidelines in AI development is not merely an academic exercise but a necessity for safeguarding human rights and promoting social equity. The Global AI Ethics and Governance Observatory and UNESCO's recommendations provide valuable frameworks for navigating the complexities of AI technology. By emphasizing core values and actionable policies, these guidelines foster a collaborative and inclusive approach to AI governance that seeks to maximize its benefits while mitigating associated risks. As we advance into an era dominated by AI, it is imperative that ethical considerations remain at the forefront of technological innovation, ensuring a future that prioritizes the well-being of humanity and the planet.

Core Principles of Ethical AI Guidelines

1. **Transparency and Explainability:** Transparency is crucial in ensuring that AI systems operate in a way that can be understood and scrutinized by human users and regulators. AI systems, particularly machine learning models, often operate as "black boxes," making decisions without easily explainable reasoning. Ethical AI guidelines promote the idea that AI systems must be designed to offer clear, understandable explanations for their decisions and actions. This helps build trust with users and allows for accountability.

2. **Fairness and Non-Discrimination:** One of the biggest concerns with AI is the potential for bias in decision-making processes. AI systems learn from data, and if that data reflects historical biases, these biases can become embedded in the AI's algorithms. Ethical AI guidelines require that AI systems be audited for fairness and that steps are taken to mitigate and eliminate bias. Ensuring non-discriminatory outcomes is especially important in areas like hiring, lending, and law enforcement, where biased algorithms can exacerbate existing inequalities.

3. **Accountability and Liability:** Establishing accountability is critical in the development of AI. When AI systems fail or cause harm, it must be clear who is responsible: the developer, the user, or the organization deploying the technology.

Ethical AI guidelines call for clear mechanisms of accountability, ensuring that all stakeholders understand the risks involved and have protocols in place to address any negative consequences. For instance, if an autonomous vehicle causes an accident, there should be a well-defined process for determining who or what is liable.

4. **Privacy and Data Protection:** AI systems are often fueled by vast amounts of data, much of which is personal and sensitive. Ethical AI guidelines stress the importance of protecting individuals' privacy and ensuring that data is handled in compliance with regulations like the General Data Protection Regulation (GDPR). AI systems must be designed to respect privacy rights and use data in a way that is both secure and transparent. Users should have control over their data and be informed about how it is being used.

5. **Human-Centric AI:** Ethical AI guidelines promote the notion that AI should enhance human capabilities, not replace or undermine them. AI systems should be designed with the intent of improving human welfare, ensuring that humans remain in control of critical decisions. The use of AI in areas like healthcare, education, and employment must prioritize the well-being of individuals and avoid dehumanizing or diminishing human roles in decision-making.

6. **Safety and Security:** AI technologies, particularly those operating in critical systems (e.g., healthcare, defense, and infrastructure), must be designed with rigorous safety protocols. Ethical AI guidelines emphasize that these systems should be robust, secure, and resilient to potential failures or attacks. In cases where AI-driven systems malfunction or

are subjected to cyberattacks, the consequences can be devastating. Hence, it is essential to ensure that AI is both safe to use and safeguarded from misuse.

7. **Inclusion and Accessibility:** AI systems should be accessible to all members of society, including marginalized or underserved groups. Ethical AI guidelines underscore the need for inclusivity in the design and deployment of AI systems, ensuring that the benefits of AI technologies are available to everyone and that no group is disproportionately disadvantaged by their use.

Importance of Ethical AI Guidelines

The adoption and implementation of Ethical AI Guidelines are crucial for ensuring that technological advancements and human progress go hand in hand. This will guarantee that technology is developed, deployed, and utilized for the betterment and well-being of humanity. The following points highlight the importance of Ethical AI Guidelines:

1. **Building Public Trust:** Public trust is paramount for the widespread adoption of AI technologies. If individuals or organizations believe that AI systems are unethical, unsafe, or biased, they are less likely to use them. Ethical AI guidelines help ensure that AI operates in a way that is aligned with societal values, making people feel more secure in interacting with these systems. This trust is essential for AI to achieve its full potential and to be integrated seamlessly into various industries.

2. **Preventing Harm and Abuse:** Without ethical considerations, AI technologies can be misused or developed in ways that cause harm. For example, AI-powered surveillance systems could

be used to violate privacy or suppress dissent. Ethical AI guidelines help prevent such abuses by establishing clear boundaries for acceptable use, promoting the development of AI that benefits society while minimizing potential harms.

3. **Ensuring Fairness and Equality:** As AI systems play an increasing role in decision-making processes, ensuring that these systems are fair and equitable is critical. Ethical AI guidelines provide the framework for auditing AI systems for bias and ensuring that they do not perpetuate discrimination. By embedding fairness into AI, we can help reduce inequality rather than exacerbate it.

4. **Legal and Regulatory Compliance:** Ethical AI guidelines also help organizations comply with existing legal frameworks and anticipate future regulations. Laws like GDPR in Europe or the California Consumer Privacy Act (CCPA) in the United States already impose strict rules on how data is handled, and these regulations will likely evolve as AI becomes more prevalent. Ethical guidelines provide a proactive approach to ensuring that AI systems comply with such regulations, avoiding potential legal risks.

5. **Fostering Innovation and Responsible AI Development:** Some may fear that ethical guidelines will stifle innovation, but in reality, they provide a roadmap for responsible development. By adhering to ethical principles, organizations can innovate in ways that are socially beneficial and sustainable. Ethical AI development also opens up new avenues for innovation, such as developing systems that are more explainable, transparent, and fair.

6. **Global Harmonization:** AI is a global technology, and ethical AI guidelines play an essential role in creating a common framework for its development and use. By establishing widely accepted principles, ethical guidelines help create consistency across different regions and sectors. This is especially important as countries and organizations work together on cross-border issues like cybersecurity, data privacy, and global commerce.

7. **Addressing Societal Concerns:** As AI takes on more complex roles in areas like law enforcement, healthcare, and transportation, ethical guidelines ensure that the broader societal implications are taken into account. For example, in healthcare, AI-driven systems should be designed to respect patient autonomy, ensure informed consent, and prioritize patient welfare. Ethical AI guidelines serve as a safeguard, ensuring that AI does not undermine key societal values such as justice, autonomy, and human dignity.

Ethical AI guidelines are not just a theoretical exercise; they are essential for ensuring that AI technologies are developed and deployed in ways that are beneficial to society. By adhering to ethical principles such as transparency, fairness, accountability, and inclusivity, organizations can help build public trust, prevent harm, and promote the responsible use of AI. As AI continues to evolve and become more integrated into daily life, the importance of ethical guidelines will only grow, making them a cornerstone of the AI-driven future.

Data Governance Policies in AI-IoT Ecosystems: Data Ownership, Consent, and Protection

The intersection of Artificial Intelligence (AI) and the Internet of Things (IoT) has revolutionized industries by creating ecosystems that generate and analyze massive volumes of data. This interconnectedness has introduced a range of challenges, particularly around data governance, with issues such as data ownership, user consent, and data protection becoming critical points of concern. Developing comprehensive governance policies in these areas is essential to maintain trust, uphold ethical standards, and ensure security within AI-IoT ecosystems.

Data Ownership

The concept of data ownership is one of the most complex issues within AI-IoT ecosystems. As devices collect and process data from various sources—ranging from personal user data to industrial machine outputs—the question of who owns that data becomes multifaceted. Traditional ownership models are being challenged as individuals, companies, and even machines contribute to the generation of data.

In many cases, IoT devices gather data continuously and automatically, raising questions about the degree of control individuals or entities should have over this information. Organizations need to develop clear legal frameworks that delineate ownership rights in a way that balances the interests of all stakeholders. For example, while a company might own the hardware or infrastructure, individuals may retain ownership over personal data, such as health metrics or behavioral data. Establishing these frameworks helps prevent data monopolization, ensuring that users are aware of their rights and that ownership is fairly distributed.

Moreover, machine-generated data—a rapidly growing segment—presents new legal challenges, as the outputs from autonomous systems are not as clearly defined in terms of ownership. Governments and industries must work together to establish guidelines for handling this type of data to avoid disputes over proprietary rights and usage, especially when multiple organizations are involved in developing, deploying, or using AI-IoT systems.

Consent Mechanisms

The acquisition of consent is another essential pillar of data governance in AI-IoT ecosystems. As IoT devices become ubiquitous in everyday life, users often engage with them in ways that may not be entirely transparent or obvious. Many devices operate continuously in the background, collecting data without active user interaction. Ensuring that users have provided informed, explicit consent for data collection, processing, and sharing is a legal and ethical necessity.

However, achieving this transparency is challenging. AI-IoT ecosystems are often designed to function seamlessly, making it difficult for users to understand how their data is being collected and used. To address this, organizations must develop user-friendly consent mechanisms that clearly explain how data will be utilized across the ecosystem. This includes enabling granular control over data-sharing preferences, allowing users to selectively opt into or out of certain data practices, while also ensuring that users can revoke consent easily if they choose to withdraw from the system.

In addition to improving transparency, organizations should focus on building trust through proactive communication about data usage. Privacy notices, data dashboards, and real-time feedback mechanisms are some tools that can help users stay informed about how their data is handled. Ensuring that consent processes are dynamic—updating users as new data collection or processing methods are introduced—is crucial in AI-IoT environments where technologies evolve rapidly.

Data Protection and Security

The immense volumes of data generated by AI-IoT ecosystems also require robust data protection policies. The interconnected nature of these systems creates multiple points of vulnerability, which could be exploited through cyberattacks, breaches, or unauthorized data access. As AI-IoT ecosystems often deal with sensitive personal, financial, or industrial data, the potential risks from inadequate protection measures are vast, ranging from individual privacy violations to large-scale disruptions in critical infrastructure.

To safeguard data, organizations must implement end-to-end security measures across the entire lifecycle of data—starting from its collection to storage, processing, and eventual disposal. Encryption protocols, secure authentication mechanisms, and real-time monitoring systems must be standard practice in AI-IoT environments. Moreover, organizations should deploy advanced threat detection systems that can quickly identify and respond to vulnerabilities, including those that may arise from the integration of new devices or third-party services.

Compliance with global data protection standards like the General Data Protection Regulation (GDPR) is critical in ensuring that organizations meet legal requirements while maintaining the highest levels of security. AI-IoT systems must also be resilient to cyberattacks, incorporating fail-safe mechanisms that can mitigate risks in the event of a breach. Data anonymization and minimization strategies should be employed to limit the amount of sensitive data stored and processed, reducing potential harm in the event of unauthorized access.

Further, policymakers should ensure that accountability mechanisms are in place, enabling individuals or organizations to challenge improper data use and seek redress. These mechanisms should include audit trails, allowing for comprehensive tracking of how data is used across AI-IoT ecosystems, and impact assessments to evaluate the potential risks associated with data handling practices.

Global Harmonization and Cross-Border Data Flow

As AI-IoT ecosystems expand globally, ensuring the harmonization of data governance policies across jurisdictions becomes increasingly important. Cross-border data flows are essential to the functioning of global AI-IoT systems, but varying regulations around data protection, ownership, and consent can lead to fragmentation, making compliance complex and resource-intensive for organizations operating in multiple regions.

Countries need to work towards developing international standards and best practices for AI-IoT governance. Collaborative efforts, such as multilateral agreements and participation in global governance bodies, will play a crucial role in establishing unified frameworks that respect local regulatory differences while promoting innovation and maintaining robust data protection standards.

The governance of data within AI-IoT ecosystems is a dynamic and evolving challenge, requiring continuous adaptation to technological advancements and legal shifts. Addressing the core issues of data ownership, user consent, and data protection is essential for creating transparent, secure, and fair AI-IoT environments. By developing comprehensive and flexible governance policies, organizations can build trust, foster innovation, and mitigate risks, ultimately contributing to the ethical and sustainable growth of AI-IoT ecosystems. As these technologies continue to advance, proactive and collaborative governance approaches will be key to balancing the immense potential of AI-IoT with the need to protect individual rights and societal well-being.

Global Perspectives on AI-IoT Policy Design

As the world becomes increasingly connected through Artificial Intelligence (AI) and the Internet of Things (IoT), the need for cohesive and effective policy frameworks has become more pressing. Each nation and region approaches AI-IoT policy design differently, shaped by their economic goals, cultural contexts, regulatory environments, and existing technological infrastructures. This growing diversity of approaches provides critical insights into the challenges and opportunities of regulating emerging technologies.

1. United States: A Balance Between Innovation and Regulatory Oversight

In the United States, the approach to AI and IoT policy is primarily market-driven, encouraging private-sector innovation while maintaining light regulatory touch. However, recent developments have signaled a shift toward more structured oversight in response to growing concerns about data privacy, cybersecurity, and algorithmic bias. The United States has relied on industry-developed standards like the National Institute of Standards and Technology (NIST) guidelines to manage AI risk, and frameworks such as the Federal Trade Commission (FTC) guidelines for data protection.

The growing influence of California's Consumer Privacy Act (CCPA) and the evolving American Data Privacy Protection Act indicate a push towards harmonizing privacy laws across the nation. Moreover, AI governance is becoming a topic of national security and competitiveness, with the U.S. initiatives like the National AI Initiative Act of 2020, aiming to ensure the country leads in AI development while mitigating risks associated with AI and IoT systems. Nevertheless, this approach still encourages market-led innovations and light regulation to avoid stifling technological advancements, while addressing increasing concerns over privacy and accountability.

2. European Union: Rigorous Regulations Rooted in Ethical AI

The European Union takes a comprehensive, regulatory-heavy approach to AI and IoT policy, emphasizing the protection of human rights, privacy, and sustainability. The General Data Protection Regulation (GDPR) remains one of the world's most robust frameworks for data privacy and protection, ensuring that organizations handling personal data, including in AI-IoT applications, adhere to strict standards. The EU's vision for AI, encapsulated in the Artificial Intelligence Act, aims to classify AI systems into risk categories, including minimal risk, limited risk, and high risk. High-risk applications, such as those in healthcare, law enforcement, and transportation, are subject to stringent regulatory oversight.

The EU prioritizes transparency, fairness, and accountability in AI-IoT systems and actively promotes human-centric AI that ensures technology serves the greater good of society. Ethics-by-design and privacy-by-design are key principles embedded in the regulatory framework, aiming to ensure inclusivity, avoid discrimination, and protect citizens from potential harm. Additionally, the EU emphasizes environmental sustainability, recognizing the energy consumption of AI-IoT systems and promoting green, energy-efficient innovations. The emphasis on trustworthy AI and data governance makes Europe a leader in AI-IoT ethics and regulation, setting a precedent for responsible technological development worldwide.

3. China: Innovation within a Controlled and Regulated Ecosystem

China's AI-IoT policy framework is fundamentally state-driven, prioritizing national security, surveillance, and economic advancement. The Chinese government has heavily invested in AI-IoT to bolster smart city development, public security, and industrial efficiency. China's Made in China 2025 initiative and Next Generation Artificial Intelligence Development Plan underscore the country's commitment to becoming a world leader in AI by 2030.

Chinese policies on AI-IoT are tightly intertwined with data governance. The Cybersecurity Law of China and Data Security Law grant the government significant control over data collection, storage, and usage, particularly when it involves national interests. This centralized approach ensures rapid implementation of AI-IoT technologies but has raised concerns regarding citizens' privacy and individual freedoms. China's Social Credit System is a notable example of how AI and IoT are used for surveillance and social governance, which contrasts sharply with the privacy-focused models in Europe and North America. Despite concerns, China's model has achieved widespread technological deployment, including advances in smart cities, AI surveillance, and autonomous systems.

4. Japan: Technological Advancement with Ethical Oversight

Japan's approach to AI-IoT policy is rooted in its vision of Society 5.0, an initiative that integrates AI and IoT technologies into every aspect of life to solve social challenges, such as an aging population and labor shortages. Japan's AI-IoT policy is uniquely focused on using technology to enhance human well-being while maintaining ethical standards. The AI Strategy 2021, developed by Japan's Cabinet Office, emphasizes the creation of human-centric AI that adheres to ethical principles like transparency, fairness, and inclusivity.

Japan also emphasizes international collaboration and regulatory harmonization, recognizing that AI-IoT applications transcend national borders. The country's policies promote data privacy, cybersecurity, and ethical AI, with particular attention to the risks associated with bias in AI algorithms. Japan's balance between technological innovation and ethical oversight ensures that AI-IoT systems are aligned with societal goals, such as enhancing quality of life and supporting sustainable development.

5. India: AI-IoT for Inclusive Growth

India's AI-IoT policy design is geared toward inclusive development and economic empowerment. India's National Strategy for AI, or AI for All, envisions AI as a tool for addressing pressing social challenges, including healthcare, education, agriculture, and public infrastructure. The government prioritizes affordable and accessible technologies, ensuring that AI-IoT solutions cater to low-resource environments and rural communities.

India is also working on comprehensive data governance frameworks, exemplified by the Personal Data Protection Bill (PDPB), which seeks to protect citizens' personal data while enabling innovation. However, India faces challenges related to digital infrastructure, data literacy, and regulatory capacity, particularly in rural regions. AI and IoT development in India is closely linked to the country's broader Digital India vision, aiming to transform India into a digitally empowered society. India's AI-IoT policy design emphasizes collaboration with both domestic industries and international stakeholders, focusing on creating frameworks that ensure non-discrimination, data privacy, and sustainable growth.

6. AI-IoT Policy Design in Pakistan: A Global Perspective

Pakistan is gradually focusing on building a comprehensive AI-IoT policy framework as part of its broader Digital Pakistan initiative. This framework aims to foster innovation across sectors like agriculture, healthcare, and energy, while addressing challenges related to governance, data privacy, and ethical use.

The Personal Data Protection Bill (PDPB) forms the backbone of Pakistan's data governance efforts, but AI-IoT ecosystems bring new complexities, including issues around data ownership, cross-border flows, and privacy concerns. Clear policies will be necessary to ensure the ethical use of AI, aligned with global frameworks like UNESCO's Recommendation on the Ethics of AI.

Economic opportunities, especially in agriculture and energy, can significantly benefit from AI-IoT integration. However, regulatory and ethical considerations remain crucial to avoid bias, data misuse, and human rights violations. Aligning with global standards such as the

GDPR and engaging in international dialogues will enable Pakistan to advance its AI-IoT ambitions responsibly.

To foster innovation, Pakistan must prioritize workforce development, research, and collaborations with global tech players. With a focus on ethical AI and global alignment, Pakistan can harness AI-IoT technologies to spur socio-economic growth while maintaining data sovereignty and human rights.

7. Canada: A Global Advocate for Ethical and Inclusive AI

Canada's approach to AI-IoT policy design emphasizes ethical AI, fairness, and inclusivity. With a strong focus on responsible AI development, Canada has positioned itself as a global leader in promoting the ethical use of AI. The Pan-Canadian AI Strategy highlights the importance of developing AI systems that respect human rights and adhere to ethical principles. Canada's policies promote transparency, accountability, and public trust, ensuring that AI and IoT systems are fair and inclusive.

Canada also emphasizes international collaboration through partnerships like the Global Partnership on AI (GPAI), which encourages shared global governance of AI technologies. Canada's AI-IoT policies highlight non-discrimination, bias mitigation, and socio-economic equality, ensuring that AI's benefits are distributed equitably across society. Additionally, data protection and privacy laws ensure that personal data collected through AI-IoT systems is safeguarded, reflecting a balanced approach between innovation and regulation.

8. Africa: Developing AI-IoT Frameworks for Sustainable Growth

African countries are at an early stage of AI-IoT policy development, with a focus on inclusive growth and capacity building. The African Union's AI strategy underscores the importance of AI for development, emphasizing how AI and IoT can help address the continent's specific challenges, including healthcare, agriculture, and education. However, many African nations face significant barriers in terms of digital infrastructure, data governance, and regulatory capacity.

To address these challenges, African governments are working on frameworks that focus on data sovereignty, ensuring that AI-IoT technologies serve local interests while promoting equitable access to technology. Collaborative efforts with global organizations and private sectors are critical in shaping Africa's AI-IoT future, focusing on sustainability, economic development, and social inclusion. By prioritizing ethical AI development and capacity building, African countries aim to leapfrog into the Fourth Industrial Revolution while avoiding the pitfalls of inequitable technological growth.

9. AI-IoT Policy Design in Saudi Arabia

Saudi Arabia's AI-IoT policy design is driven by its Vision 2030 initiative, aimed at transforming the country into a knowledge-based economy. The Saudi Data and Artificial Intelligence Authority (SDAIA) and the National Strategy for Data and AI (NSDAI) are central to this effort, focusing on innovation, economic diversification, and job creation through large-scale projects like NEOM. As energy efficiency requirements are emereging as the crucial building blocks to have the AI-IoT evolution, Saudi Arabia has positioned itself well as one of the Central Hub for AI global revolution and deployment.

Key elements of Saudi AI-IoT policy include:

1. **Data Governance:** The Personal Data Protection Law (PDPL) sets guidelines for data privacy and security, ensuring AI-IoT applications protect personal data, similar to the GDPR.

2. **Cybersecurity:** The National Cybersecurity Authority (NCA) enforces cybersecurity measures to protect critical infrastructure and data-driven systems, addressing the risks posed by AI-IoT technologies.

3. **Ethics:** Saudi Arabia promotes ethical AI development, aligning with Islamic values and global best practices. SDAIA emphasizes fairness, transparency, and accountability in AI projects.

4. **Global Collaboration:** The Kingdom actively engages in international forums like the Global Partnership on AI (GPAI) to align its AI-IoT policies with global standards.

Saudi Arabia's AI-IoT policy aims to foster innovation, enhance public services, and ensure ethical and secure development of emerging technologies as part of its Vision 2030 goals.

The global perspectives on AI-IoT policy design reflect a diverse landscape of regulatory approaches, driven by economic, ethical, and societal priorities. While countries like the United States and China promote rapid innovation with varying degrees of state control, regions like the European Union and Canada prioritize ethics, human rights, and transparency. Japan and India provide valuable models of how AI-IoT can be used to address social challenges and promote inclusive growth, while Africa is emerging as a key player focused on sustainable development and ethical AI governance. As AI and IoT continue to shape the future, the importance of globally harmonized, ethical, and responsible policy frameworks will only grow, ensuring that technology serves the global good.

Call for Proactive Policy Design:

The Importance of Continuous Dialogue and Inclusive Policy Frameworks

The exponential rise of artificial intelligence (AI) and the Internet of Things (IoT) has reshaped modern society, impacting every sector from healthcare and education to manufacturing and public administration. As these technologies become further entrenched in daily life, a clear, proactive approach to policy design becomes not just beneficial but imperative. Such an approach moves beyond the reactive models of the past, where policies were created only after challenges became apparent. Instead, proactive policy design involves anticipating both the risks and opportunities that AI and IoT present, allowing for strategic interventions that safeguard public interest, foster innovation, and support sustainable growth.

In addition to safeguarding against risks, proactive policy design lays the groundwork for promoting innovation. In environments where policies are transparent and forward-looking, businesses and technology developers find the stability and clarity they need to invest in and test new ideas. Proactive policies allow governments to establish standards and expectations for AI and

IoT, particularly in sensitive areas such as data privacy, cybersecurity, and human rights, giving businesses a roadmap for compliance while they focus on innovating. By creating this balanced framework, governments can promote a regulatory environment that encourages responsible experimentation and investment, leading to economic growth and positioning countries as leaders in the global tech landscape.

Continuous dialogue is a central component of effective policy design in this domain, as no single entity holds all the insights necessary to address the complexities of AI and IoT. Policymakers need to engage regularly with industry experts, academics, consumer advocates, and civil society groups to understand how technologies are used, what challenges arise, and how these challenges impact various sectors and communities. Such dialogue ensures policies remain relevant and effective, preventing scenarios where regulations become obsolete or, conversely, overly restrictive, stifling technological growth.

By fostering this ongoing exchange of ideas, governments can gather up-to-date insights, respond to the nuances of emerging technologies, and adjust policies as needed, all while building trust among stakeholders. Transparent, regular communication signals to the public that their voices are considered, addressing concerns around safety, privacy, and fairness.

Inclusivity in policy design goes beyond merely gathering a range of viewpoints; it demands a structure where all stakeholders, especially marginalized or vulnerable populations, have meaningful input. AI and IoT technologies often carry the risk of amplifying existing social inequalities if not designed and implemented with equity in mind. For instance, AI systems may reflect biases in their training data, leading to discriminatory outcomes in areas like hiring, lending, and law enforcement. IoT, while facilitating connectivity, can also widen the digital divide, as those without access to technology are left further behind. Inclusive policy frameworks make sure these issues are addressed from the outset by including diverse perspectives, ensuring that the benefits of technological advances are broadly distributed.

Ethics must also be deeply embedded in these inclusive policies. As AI and IoT have far-reaching impacts on personal privacy, autonomy, and even personal agency, ethical considerations must be at the heart of policy frameworks. Prioritizing fairness, accountability, transparency, and respect for privacy not only aligns technology with societal values but also helps prevent misuse or harmful consequences. For instance, policies might require transparency in AI decision-making processes, allowing individuals to understand and contest decisions made by AI algorithms that affect them.

Policies that mandate ethical standards in AI and IoT development cultivate public trust, a critical factor for adoption and responsible growth.

Furthermore, inclusive policy frameworks must consider the future of work in an AI-IoT-driven world. As automation and intelligent systems reshape job markets, proactive policies should address reskilling and upskilling needs. Governments can invest in educational programs, vocational training, and workforce development to prepare individuals for careers in an increasingly digital economy. Such policies not only protect workers from displacement but also ensure a pipeline of skilled professionals who can contribute to and benefit from technological progress.

A call for proactive, inclusive, and ethical policy design is ultimately a call to shape a future that is resilient, innovative, and just. In the absence of forward-looking policies, societies risk falling into a reactive stance, where issues of privacy, fairness, and equity are only addressed after harm has occurred. Conversely, when governments adopt proactive and inclusive policy frameworks, they establish a social contract that upholds the values of equity, opportunity, and public trust. Such frameworks do not merely regulate technology; they define a vision of technological progress that aligns with the common good, balancing the drive for innovation with an unwavering commitment to humanity.

As we stand at the threshold of an AI and IoT-driven future, proactive policy design is the bridge that will guide us forward with wisdom and inclusivity. This approach not only prepares society for the technological challenges ahead but also nurtures a vision of progress that is ethical, equitable, and inclusive for all. By championing continuous dialogue, inclusivity, and ethical standards, policymakers can create a resilient framework for AI and IoT that prioritizes people, fosters innovation, and ensures that the benefits of technological advancements are shared widely across society.

Final Thoughts on Navigating AI-IoT Integration

As artificial intelligence (AI) and the Internet of Things (IoT) continue to evolve, their integration offers boundless potential to reshape industries, redefine social structures, and elevate standards of living. Yet, navigating this integration responsibly requires that governments, businesses, and societies embrace a holistic, proactive approach to policy design that anticipates challenges, fosters innovation, and safeguards public welfare. The future outlook for AI-IoT integration in policy is filled with both promise and complexity.

When approached thoughtfully, these technologies can advance sustainable development, enhance public services, and strengthen economies. However, achieving these outcomes requires a forward-looking policy approach that prioritizes inclusivity, ethics, and resilience.

In the coming years, AI-IoT policy will likely shift toward adaptive frameworks that allow policies to evolve with technology, rather than remain static. This adaptability will be critical as new use cases and unforeseen ethical questions continue to arise. A central aspect of these adaptive frameworks will be the establishment of ethical guidelines that govern how AI and IoT are designed, deployed, and regulated. Issues of data privacy, transparency in AI decision-making, and safeguards against biases must be carefully embedded into policy frameworks to ensure that technology remains aligned with human values. Furthermore, these policies must promote digital literacy and equitable access, enabling all communities to benefit from and contribute to the AI-IoT landscape. In particular, vulnerable and marginalized groups must be considered, as failing to do so could exacerbate existing inequalities and digital divides.

For policymakers, the challenge will be balancing regulation with the flexibility needed to encourage innovation. Too much regulation could stifle technological growth, while too little could leave society vulnerable to privacy invasions, economic inequalities, and even social disruption. Therefore, a "sandbox" approach, where AI and IoT applications are tested in controlled environments, can serve as a valuable tool, allowing regulators to assess the societal impacts of these technologies in real time before broad deployment. Additionally, partnerships between government, industry, and academia will become increasingly important, fostering a collaborative approach that can draw on a diverse range of expertise to tackle the multifaceted challenges of AI-IoT integration.

The broader implications of AI-IoT integration for society are profound. Smart cities, personalized healthcare, precision agriculture, and connected industries are just a few examples of how this integration could lead to substantial improvements in quality of life, environmental sustainability, and economic productivity. However, as these technologies reshape social norms and interactions, they also raise questions about individual agency, data ownership, and autonomy. Thoughtful policy design will be crucial in navigating these shifts, ensuring that the benefits of AI-IoT integration are realized while protecting human rights and preserving societal values.

Ultimately, navigating AI-IoT integration is about building a future that harmonizes technological innovation with ethical considerations, inclusivity, and public well-being. By fostering adaptive policies, maintaining continuous dialogue, and committing to ethical standards, society can harness the transformative potential of AI and IoT to create a future that is not only technologically advanced but also equitable and aligned with the common good. In doing so, we can lay the foundation for a resilient society, ready to meet the challenges and seize the opportunities of an increasingly interconnected world.

Abbreviations (A–Z)

- **AI** – Artificial Intelligence
- **AV** – Autonomous Vehicles
- **CCPA** – California Consumer Privacy Act
- **COVID** – Coronavirus Disease
- **CPS** – Cyber-Physical Systems
- **EIA** – Environmental Impact Assessment
- **EMA** – European Medicines Agency
- **ETS** – Emissions Trading System
- **EU** – European Union
- **FCA** – Financial Conduct Authority
- **FDA** – Food and Drug Administration
- **FTC** – Federal Trade Commission
- **GDP** – Gross Domestic Product
- **GDPR** – General Data Protection Regulation
- **GPAI** – Global Partnership on Artificial Intelligence
- **IGF** – Internet Governance Forum
- **IP** – Internet Protocol
- **ITU** – International Telecommunication Union
- **MIL** – Media and Information Literacy
- **NCA** – National Cybersecurity Authority

- **NEOM** – A planned cross-border city in the Tabuk Province of northwestern Saudi Arabia
- **NHTSA** – National Highway Traffic Safety Administration
- **NIST** – National Institute of Standards and Technology
- **NSDAI** – National Strategy for Data and Artificial Intelligence (Saudi Arabia)
- **PDPB** – Personal Data Protection Bill (India)
- **PDPL** – Personal Data Protection Law (various regions)
- **RAM** – Random Access Memory
- **RFID** – Radio Frequency Identification
- **SDAIA** – Saudi Data and Artificial Intelligence Authority
- **SMART** – Specific, Measurable, Achievable, Relevant, Time-bound
- **UAE** – United Arab Emirates
- **UK** – United Kingdom
- **UNESCO** – United Nations Educational, Scientific and Cultural Organization
- **US** – United States

www.ingramcontent.com/pod-product-compliance
Lightning Source LLC
LaVergne TN
LVHW052055060326
832903LV00061B/974